WORDS OF PRAISE

Everybody knows that healthy eating and fitness are really important. The problem is that talking about them is often both fear- and shame-inducing. Happily, in *It Began in the Garden*, Heidi Zwart finds a way to talk about this important subject without the platitudes and "you're doing it wrong" tone that often characterizes conversations on health. Her advice is simple and practical, and she writes from a faith perspective that simultaneously clarifies and enriches the "why" behind healthy lifestyle choices. And once we understand the "why," the "how" becomes much clearer. Sometimes moving forward requires looking back.

- **Dr. Jim Beilby,** professor of Theology,
Bethel University, St. Paul, MN

Reading Heidi's book was like sitting down for coffee with a trusted friend. Her openness in sharing her own struggles with weight and body image makes her not only a great coach but also a great teammate. The nutrition and wellness advice Heidi shares is spot-on—simple in its approach, but profound in its application. The grace and encouragement Heidi offers along the way inspires a can-do attitude that will put readers on the path toward real and lasting lifestyle change.

- **Cindy Mather**, registered dietitian

It Began in the Garden is well written, creative, punchy, and readable. Heidi's warmth and heart for transformation shines through each lesson.

- **Bob Merritt**, senior pastor, Eagle Brook Church

Do you struggle putting healthy eating habits into place? Does the task seem insurmountable? Then you'll love Heidi's approach. *It Began In The Garden* is about putting small steps into place to change the way you think about fitness, health, and who you are in Christ. Filled with Biblical wisdom, this book offers a simple and sacred approach to living healthy.

- **Jo Bender**, host of *Connecting Faith* on Faith Radio Network

Heidi takes a whole approach to health, connecting mind, body, and spirit in ways that not only encourage us to be healthy, but also to be whole. She understands the foundations of growth and change, and her expertise and compassion make it easy to see why she's such an effective coach. In *It Began In The Garden*, you'll value her honest insights and wisdom as she encourages you to make the kinds of small changes that produce big and lasting results! With Heidi as your guide, you'll have an experienced coach to motivate you, and a relatable, trusted friend and counselor to encourage you along the way in your journey toward health.

- **Kristen Paulsen**, pastor and writer

Put away the diet books and the how-to books and kick back and savor this one instead. Heidi will take you on a soul-soothing search for the balance and patience you need to make positive changes stick. Habits. Good habits. Recognizing them, developing them, maintaining them is king in this beautifully written book. Prepare to be captivated by Heidi's poise, humor, and spiritual insight. *It Began in the Garden* will be a bright spot in your journey to a healthier—inside and out—you!

> - **Margie Broman**, co-author of *Bridge to Teen: Biblically Bridging the Gap Between Childhood and Adolescence*

In memory of my grandma Verna,
whose love for words is my heritage.

CONTENTS

FOREWORD

Health matters. From an early age, I committed to being physically fit. It's one of my top-five life values. I decided early on that whatever else happened in my life, staying healthy would be one of the keys to living a better life.

It's not always easy. Every day after work, I come to a stop sign. If I go straight ahead over a bridge, I drive home to a warm house, a warm meal, and a relaxing evening with my wife. If I turn right onto the freeway, I drive ten miles to the gym and endure a brutal workout before showering and heading home. Straight ahead leads to comfort; turning right leads to torture. Every day, I face that decision, and five days a week, I turn right. Why? Because if I keep going straight, I can't achieve my goals. I can't do what I was made to do. As hard as it is to turn right, the payoff is worth it. I'm stronger and healthier, I have more energy, and I'm in a better mood when I get home (and my wife is grateful for that!).

The value I've put on my health drives this daily decision and determines where I go and what I do. It narrows my focus and eliminates competing options. It has played a significant part in my ability to lead a church from 350 to 22,000. Without prioritizing my health, this may not have been possible. It continues to be part of what keeps me energized and mobile enough to continue leading this growing church. Even though I committed to my health long ago, it's still a daily decision to live by this value. The struggle is real. And it started long before you and I were born.

The lessons health and wellness coach Heidi Zwart talks about in *It Began in the Garden* don't promise a magic pill for better health, but they do offer a biblical understanding of the origin of our struggle and how to overcome it with small, daily decisions. The principles found within this book are grounded in the biblical account of Adam and Eve and how one simple decision created the challenges we face every day, not only in life but in our health. They also flow out of the life and wisdom of a respected friend and colleague.

I've known Heidi for many years and have witnessed her authenticity and wisdom as a respected member of our church board. Heidi's one of the best, most trustworthy people I know. She has a genuine passion for reaching people for Christ so that their lives are transformed. The words on the pages of this book flow from that heart.

Not only do you need this book, but someone in your life needs it, too. Your health matters. Their health matters. Your legacy, the life you were meant to live, is at stake. You may not be able to change the beginning of your story. None of us are. But you can start to script a better future.

Decide today to start writing. It's never too late to write a healthier ending.

Bob Merritt
Senior Pastor, Eagle Brook Church

INTRODUCTION

The world of nutrition and fitness is confusing. A quick scroll through your social media accounts or television channels is proof. We aren't lacking expert advice or celebrities promising a once-and-for-all weight-loss solution. Dozens and dozens of products and plans promise success. Advertisements, infomercials, and stories of trusted friends barrage us with options. And lots and lots of noise.

The side effect is confusion. Paralysis. We don't know what to do or who to believe, so we do nothing. Or we try, fail, and become even more discouraged that yet another plan didn't work. We blame ourselves for our lack of willpower or self-control. Or we berate the program for being too hard or too complicated. We remain frustrated and discouraged.

This is *not* another one of those weight-loss plans disguised as a book. Inside these pages, you won't find the magic pill to shed pounds quickly once and for all. This book has no formulas to follow, meal plans to build, calories to count, or points to track. I don't believe in a one-size-fits-all nutrition or exercise program. There is no mathematical calculation for success. If that's what you're looking for, this book isn't for you.

I understand your desire for a once-and-for-all solution. I get it. I've battled the weight-loss roller coaster, too. I still fight body image issues. And I struggle with depression and anxiety at times. In search of a fix, I've even become a certified nutrition and fitness coach to try to figure it all out. Honestly, sometimes I'm just as confused and frustrated as you.

But I've learned some lessons along the way. I've discovered some common challenges we face and methods to overcome them. As a master's level counselor, nutrition coach, life coach, and personal trainer, I've been fortunate to help hundreds of people make healthy life changes. These changes don't happen overnight, though. It isn't a quick-fix solution. But with patience and practice, they get unstuck.

They lose weight.
They eat better.
They work out smarter.
They sleep better.
They are less stressed.
They believe in themselves again.

Just like you, they wanted a healthier future. They knew they needed to make some changes to make that happen, so they went to work applying many of the methods you'll learn in this book. If that sounds like the kind of life you want to live, then this book is for you.

Everyone is unique. We have different metabolisms, hormones, and predispositions toward disease. We are different ages, genders, and ethnicities. Add in lifestyle choices like jobs, family, social commitments, church, and sports, and we've got a recipe for uncommon ground. All of it impacts our quality of life and the time we dedicate to our health.

Despite our uniqueness, however, we also share some common struggles around food and fitness. Around life in general, really. We've probably all wondered at times if there's something wrong with us when we can't exercise consistently or eat the things we know are good for our bodies. We've been struggling with this for a long, long time.

In truth, we were destined for this fight. We didn't have a choice. Way back in the very beginning, Earth's original inhabitants, Adam and Eve, *did* have a choice. And they didn't make a very good one. With their not-so-great decision about a piece of fruit came the struggle we continue to fight today. We carry the pain and consequences of the baggage they left for us. They wrote the opening line of a story we can't rewrite. That's the bad news.

But there's good news, too. Though we can't change the beginning, we *can* write the rest of the story. We've been given the opening sentence of chapter 1. That's it. We can choose a different middle and ending. Even if we haven't written an ideal story so far or made great choices to this point, there's still time to write a better one for a healthier future.

So, if you're ready to start writing a better story through simple, practical changes, keep reading. If you're ready and willing to look at food and exercise differently, through the lens of a familiar story that happened long, long ago in a beautiful garden, this is for you. You will be encouraged and equipped to make practical changes in your day-to-day life. And more importantly, connect to why it matters.

Warning. You *may* drop a size along the way or see the number on that scale finally move. You may see some improvements to your inner health, too. Better choices lead to better health. Small changes lead to a better future. A better story.

Each chapter in this book is a lesson. Weaving the biblical story of Adam and Eve throughout the chapters, we will see how *one* choice about a piece of fruit impacted the health battle we have today. We will look at what went wrong and how we can fall into the same choices today unless we choose differently. Though we can't undo that first, fateful decision in the garden or escape the consequences, we can learn from it and move toward a better choice. Be forewarned that the appeal, the desire, to follow in their footsteps is strong. The whisper of the serpent is very real. We make a choice to respond to or ignore his voice in favor of God's voice of truth. Every single day. One decision at a time.

Using examples from both personal and professional experience, we'll take a closer look at desire, temptation, personal responsibility, body image, shame, and blame and how each impacts our choices about food and exercise. You will be encouraged with small, practical steps to make better choices than our garden-dwelling, fig-leaf-wearing ancestors did. You will have takeaway principles and clear guidance to reclaim your health. Not all at once, but little by little with time and practice.

I'm suggesting a few options to fully digest this book. Choose the one that will uniquely work for you, knowing your learning style, lifestyle, and reading preference. Or use a hybrid of these options to help you meet your own personal goals.

1. *Read this from cover to cover, at your own pace. Each chapter has an application section at the end of the book that you can use as you like. Grab a notebook and think through the questions, writing them down for your own personal growth.*

2. *Recruit a friend to read this book with you. Pick a chapter a week to discuss together and hold each other accountable for making healthy life changes. Life is better when it's shared.*

3. *Use this book as a small group study. As you make your way through the chapters week by week, gather together to discuss the weekly topic and support each other in your quest to live a life of health.*

Whichever option you choose, when you are finished reading this book, you will be equipped with tools for change. The small, incremental decisions and daily choices you start practicing create a ripple that, over time, becomes a gigantic tidal wave of change. What you do today impacts your tomorrow. And the next day. And the next day. So are you ready to choose today?

Your future is waiting. The rest of your story begins now.

LESSON 1:

FOOD FIGHTS ARE MESSY

In the beginning was an apple. A beautiful, perfect fruit. Unblemished. Enticing. And forbidden.

In the beginning was a man. And a woman. Beautiful, perfect people. Unblemished. Enticed. And tempted.

And that's where perfection came to an ugly end. Back in the very first garden, a simple piece of fruit and a rash decision led to devastating results. Life-changing results. Not just for Adam and Eve but for you and me, too.

Some of you may know this story in detail but maybe haven't looked at it from this perspective before. Even those without a Bible background likely know the main characters and how the story plays out. Regardless of your background or belief system, this story matters. Why? Because it's impacted everything that's happened since. Everything. Including our health.

Simply put, Adam and Eve made a mess. The food fight of all food fights. Imagine having access to everything you ever wanted and needed. Fruits, vegetables, meats, grains, and plants. Pure, natural, healthy, straight-from-the-mouth-of-God-created nourishment. Trees dripping with an abundance of life-giving, ideal nutrients. The ground bursting with fresh vegetables, berries, and herbs.

No pesticides, toxins, or spots on the apple. Everything was organic, non-GMO (no genetic modifications), and locally grown.

> God said, "Look! I have given you every seed-bearing plant throughout the earth and all the fruit trees for your food. And I have given every green plant as food for all the wild animals, the birds in the sky, and the small animals that scurry along the ground—everything that has life." (Genesis 1:29–30)

What a gift! But God wasn't finished. He took it a step further. He added a bonus. He gave Adam a dining companion and life partner. Eve was the ideal partner, perfectly designed to share the garden, the creatures of the earth, and all of life that was to come.

> Then the Lord God made a woman from the rib, and he brought her to the man. "At last!" the man exclaimed. "This one is bone from my bone, and flesh from my flesh! She will be called 'woman,' because she was taken from 'man.'" This explains why a man leaves his father and mother and is joined to his wife, and the two are united into one. (Genesis 2:22–24)

Each was created for the other. They were physical and relational complements. Each existed in complete nakedness with no shame. They didn't cover up blemishes, apologize for imperfections, or hide in the dark from each other. Imagine that! They were naked . . . but not afraid. No guilt. No baggage. No hiding. Everything was awesome. Until it wasn't.

There was *one* thing they couldn't have. One. Adam and Eve had access to 1,001 things (give or take) and only one thing to avoid. A reliable source—*the most reliable source*—

told them to stay away from that one tree, to not even flirt with it. (Well, God told *Adam* and assumed he was listening!) There was no ambiguity. No room for interpretation. He laid out the consequences if they disobeyed. Death.

> The Lord God placed the man in the Garden of Eden to tend and watch over it. But the Lord God warned him, "You may freely eat the fruit of every tree in the garden—except the tree of the knowledge of good and evil. If you eat its fruit, you are sure to die." (Genesis 2:15 17)

Yet, despite this severe warning, another voice caught their attention. Satan's voice was shrewd and trained in the art of deception. His voice twisted the words of truth and took pleasure in doing so. He didn't use a commercial or social media. He didn't use fancy images or photoshopped promises. He didn't need them. He used desire. Adam and Eve's desires.

> "You won't die!" the serpent replied to the woman. "God knows that your eyes will be opened as soon as you eat it, and you will be like God, knowing both good and evil." (Genesis 3:4-5)

Satan made a promise, too. A subtle twisting of God's promise. He proposed that divine wisdom was worth pursuing. He promised Adam and Eve what he, himself, had tried to gain and failed. He promised them the very thing that he vigorously pursued without success, a pursuit that landed him in hell. There was no doubt he knew the truth of God's warning, but misery loves company, so he became the great deceiver.

Adam and Eve *knew* what was true. God told them. They *knew* what was best. God told them that, too. In the beginning, they trusted God; he was their sole source of right and wrong, good and bad. They had no reason to question him. There was only one voice and no contradictory information to confuse them. Everything was crystal clear. They weren't barraged with hundreds of options or opinions or experts who contradicted one another. They didn't have labels to read, celebrities to emulate, or research studies to muddle through. It should have been easy.

But then that darn snake slithered in. He offered an alternative. He offered his perspective. And he was an expert in his own right. In fact, he was the leading expert in false advertising and addiction. He was about to use his power of seduction on these naïve inhabitants. He knew something Adam and Eve didn't. He knew about desire. So he preyed.

The low-hanging fruit looked *so* appealing. It looked *so* delicious. It looked *so* irresistible. The serpent's only task was to use what he knew about Adam and Eve's natures for his purposes. It didn't take much. He planted the seed of question and doubt. And Adam and Eve's minds, and hearts, spun.

How could something that beautiful be bad for me?
Will it taste different from all the other fruit?
Will one bite actually kill me?
Why would God make it if it was going to hurt me?
Is God using scare tactics?
Is God really the expert?
Why would anyone deceive me?
Maybe the snake does know best?
What could it hurt?

It was just this once . . .
Enter shame.

So she took some of the fruit and ate it. Then she gave some to her husband, who was with her, and he ate it, too. At that moment, their eyes were opened, and they suddenly felt shame at their nakedness. So they sewed fig leaves together to cover themselves. (Genesis 3:6b–7)

Swift and immediate regret engulfed them. Instantly aware of the choice they had made, they ran and hid. They were exposed and acutely aware of their bodies. They didn't like what they saw.

Enter blame.

"Who told you that you were naked?" the Lord God asked. "Have you eaten from the tree whose fruit I commanded you not to eat?" The man replied, "It was the woman you gave me who gave me the fruit, and I ate it." Then the Lord God asked the woman, "What have you done?"

"The serpent deceived me," she replied. "That's why I ate it." (Genesis 3:11–13)

Adam turned the finger on God (who created the enticement). Eve pointed the finger at the serpent (as he laughed and banked his win). Neither took responsibility for their choice. There was no do-over. No next time. No "I'll start Monday."

Then he said to the woman,
"I will sharpen the pain of your pregnancy,
  and in pain you will give birth.
And you will desire to control your husband,
  but he will rule over you."

And to the man he said,
"Since you listened to your wife and ate from the tree whose fruit I commanded you not to eat, the ground is cursed because of you.

5

*All your life you will struggle to scratch a living
from it.
It will grow thorns and thistles for you,
 though you will eat of its grains.
By the sweat of your brow
 will you have food to eat
until you return to the ground
 from which you were made.
For you were made from dust,
 and to dust you will return."* (Genesis 3:16–19)

Their choice, regardless of fault, had consequences.

Shortly before my oldest son, Drew, became a licensed driver, we purchased another car. He spent hours researching vehicles before settling on a make and model that fit his needs and our budget. He loved his car. He hauled around his goalie equipment (smelly) and his hockey friends (smellier) with great pride. He was quick to volunteer when his friends needed a ride.

One night, the details of which have never been fully disclosed, he was out pranking friends and was, predictably (at least by adult wisdom), met with retribution. As he was cruising behind the wheel, preparing for another attack, one of his intended targets got a jump on him. Pie in hand, "Joe" ran full speed at the car and let it fly directly at Drew. Harmless, right? Except the driver's-side window was open. What should have been a pretty easy cleanup turned into a sloppy, drippy mess over the dashboard, steering wheel, ceiling . . . and Drew.

Did I mention it was an apple pie? Drew spent hours cleaning up that car. On the surface, it eventually looked clean. The scrubbing took away (most) visible signs of the errant pie stunt, but pieces remained. For months, he'd find remnants in the cracks and crevices of the car's interior.

Reminders of that one night, that one decision, lingered out of sight, hidden and seemingly undetectable—but still there.

Know what happened when he left for college? *We* inherited the car. My husband, Kevin, became its primary driver. Welcoming him each time he opened the driver's-side door was a lingering odor. Beyond the obvious culprit, his own hockey reffing gear, he couldn't identify the noxious smell. In exasperation, he finally tore the car apart and found the odiferous source. Wanna guess what he found? Yep. Apple pie. Pieces of it still there, out of sight, almost a year later. Even after Drew's initial sweep and his occasional teenage-boy touch-ups, pieces escaped visual detection, but there was no doubt that they remained. They stunk.

Though Kevin had nothing to do with the pie-throwing, he lived with the daily reminder of that one decision. That one choice. He inherited the mess. That rash decision—hurling a pie at a friend for fun—led to a much bigger mess than intended. Joe's motive wasn't to cause chaos (well, maybe a little), yet it ensued anyway. Sometimes, the smallest actions lead to the biggest messes. Sometimes our choices stink.

In contrast to teenage shenanigans, the serpent, the biggest prankster of them all, *intended* harm. He knew the consequences of his pie-throwing and was giddy with anticipation. He slithered, aimed, and hit his target straight on. Dead center. And we, the entire human race, inherited the mess. And the stink.

Adam and Eve had an abundance of life-giving, nourishing options. They had plentiful food, perfect relational harmony, and ideal health. It was set before them at their fingertips. Their only rule to was avoid the *one* thing that was bad for them. The life-ending kind of bad. They chose differently, however. It's been pain in childbirth, male-female power struggles, animosity, and hard work ever since. It's easy to think we would have made a different choice. How hard could it have been to stay away from a single piece of fruit? Now, if it had been a slice of pizza . . .

The truth is we make the same choice every day. Yes, we have more than one thing to avoid. Some days it feels more like 1,001 things, but each choice is a decision with consequences. Health or pain. Abundance or toiling. Blessings or curses. Health comes through the small, good decisions we make in those moments of desire and temptation. We make choices that extend our lives instead of prematurely end them. When you want what you can't have, no matter how enticing it may be, you have a choice to make. Life or death? Simple choices lead to big things. Really big things. The consequences can be really bad, the life-changing kind of bad—or they can be really good, the life-changing kind of good.

Drew is now the primary driver of "his" car again. That car is now stocked with wet wipes because, in his own words, "You never know when an apple pie will come flying through your window again!" He learned a valuable lesson on the heels of his one impulsive decision. He didn't like cleaning up the mess. Today, he's equipped to make a different choice, but in case temptation gets the better of him, he's at least prepared to do a surface cleaning.

How do you know where to start changing the script in your own life? Where do you begin?

Here are three ways to know if you need to start cleaning up a mess:

Take a big whiff.
Start by taking an honest assessment of your current state of health. Take a really big breath in. What do you smell? What's reminding you that what you've tried so hard to

cover up isn't going to work for long? The stink can't hide forever. If it's there, it will smell funky and foul, if not today, then tomorrow. All the air freshener and deodorizer in the world can't cover the stench permanently (think spilled milk on carpet). Yuck. Dig until you find the source of the odor. Then start scrubbing and carrying wet wipes.

Be curious.

Learn from a typical two-year-old. Ask why. Over and over again. Get to the heart of the problem. Ask yourself why life isn't working right now. And more importantly, ask how it would look different if you *did* change the script. Ask yourself why you need a change. Then keep digging. The "5 Whys" was a system originally developed by Toyota Motor Corporation.[1] This process starts by asking one *why* question such as "Why do I need to make some health changes?" and then following this up with another *why* question. Then ask why again. Five times. Eventually, you will arrive at your true motivation for a cleanup.

Consider the impact.

What is your current health state costing you? What are you not able to do? What are you not fully able to experience? If this were off your plate, what would your life look like instead? What could you be freed up to do? If you feel unable to control your emotional eating or lack energy to engage with friends and family, you may need to take out the cleaning rags. If you are not able to do what God has uniquely designed you to do, it's time for a makeover.

Don't wait. Start today. God is a God of clean slates. And it's never too late for a fresh start.

*"For I am about to do something new.
See, I have already begun! Do you not see it?
I will make a pathway through the wilderness.
I will create rivers in the dry wasteland."*
—Isaiah 43:19

LESSON 2:

THERE WILL ALWAYS BE A YOGURT AISLE

Have you ever gone grocery shopping with a toddler in tow? How about a toddler and an infant? You can probably relate. There seems to be an unspoken rule that toddlers follow; choices they're presented with are *never* as appealing as the ones that are not. Shopping was a challenge in the early days with my first two boys being only fifteen months apart. Even a routine trip to the grocery store was risky. A reward (okay, if we're honest, it was a bribe) was often offered to Drew if we made it to the checkout lane without incident.

One shopping day, we had three elements combined for the perfect storm. Between Drew the toddler, Alex the colicky baby, and me the sleep-deprived mom, we were a time bomb ready to explode. I could hear the tick getting louder as we approached the yogurt aisle. Being the clever, wise mom I was, I presented Drew with two semi-nutritious options. (Life *is* all about choices after all, and I was empowering Drew to make them!) Drew would have none of it. The seemingly hundreds of other shiny, colorful yogurts available were just too enticing for him. Once he had fixed his eyes on all the other desirable options, there was no reining in his attention.

I finally laid down the ultimatum. "You can pick one of the two I'm holding, or I will pick one for you."

Boom. Detonation. Screaming commenced, tantrum ensued, and we made it home with only half of the groceries we had intended to get that day. Needless to say, Drew did not get his promised reward. Drew's desire and curiosity about that shiny packaging got the best of him. He ignored the voice that presented the best options for his health and well-being. He didn't trust that he was being guided by someone who knew what was good for him . . . and what was not (sugar-filled, nutritional nothingness). Even after a stern warning from someone who loved him and wanted the best for him, he was enticed by what he thought he was missing. He was given the opportunity to make a good choice, but he couldn't do it.

Sound familiar? The grocery store isn't exactly the Garden of Eden, but it sure can feel like it. Adam and Eve had an abundance of food set before them. An assortment of colors, flavors, shapes, and fragrances. Raspberries, strawberries, lemons, cherries, oranges, and so much more. Ready and waiting.

> *Then the Lord God planted a garden in Eden in the east, and there he placed the man he had made. The Lord God made all sorts of trees grow up from the ground—trees that were beautiful and that produced delicious fruit.* (Genesis 2:8–9a)

The packaging was perfect. The details were designed by a creative genius. A master marketer. It was an intuitive gift, not something contrived or manipulative. He used just the right shades of green, red, and yellow in harmonious design. His divine nature sought to bring pleasure to his creation.

Inside the packaging, God packed dense, perfectly blended nutrients to feed his sole inhabitants. He provided the soil and tended it perfectly so that it would keep his new friends not only alive but thriving. He heated the sun, called upon the rain, and fertilized the ground to provide an abundant harvest. These original plant foods were their core sustenance.

> *Then God said, "Look! I have given you every seed-bearing plant throughout the earth and all the fruit trees for your food. And I have given every green plant as food for all the wild animals, the birds in the sky, and the small animals that scurry along the ground—everything that has life."* (Genesis 1:29–30)

As a bonus, he added flavor. Wow. What a coup! He didn't have to do that. He could have made it bland and functional. Instead, he infused each fruit and vegetable with an explosion of flavor. He gave us taste buds that could distinguish the diverse experiences of the five basic tastes: sweet, sour, bitter, umami, and salty. He *wanted* food to give us pleasure.

And then he said, "Here. You choose." Unlike me, the controlling mother in the grocery store who wanted to limit the chaos of choice, *this* Father said, "You can have this one, or this one, or this one, or this one, or this one, or this one." He left only one option on the shelf, but they wanted *that one*. It was the *only* flavor to which God said no.

> *But the Lord God warned him, "You may freely eat the fruit of every tree in the garden—except the tree of the knowledge of good and evil. If you eat its fruit, you are sure to die."* (Genesis 2:16–17)

Dozens of choices—maybe hundreds or thousands—but they pointed and said, "I want *that* one." How often do we do the same thing? How often do we have set before us dozens and dozens of life-giving foods? Plant-based foods filled with ideal nourishment sit at our fingertips, yet we choose the enticing, man-made, food-like substances that should be labeled "off limits"? We ignore the tick. We point and choose "that one." *Boom.* The crunch from that first bite still resonates.

Most, if not all, grocery stores are set up with the produce section at the front entrance. It's almost impossible to miss. It's a true feast for the eyes. If a particular fruit or vegetable isn't appealing, there are plenty of alternatives. Don't like kale? Eat spinach. Don't like Brussels sprouts? (Me either.) Choose asparagus. Not a fan of cantaloupe? Have an apple. Not a strawberry lover? Grab some raspberries.

Think fruit has too much sugar? Hogwash. A bowl of your favorite cereal or a granola bar likely has far more sugar than a banana or an orange. A carton of Yoplait contains as much sugar as a can of Coke! And the dressing used to top your "healthy" salad can fill your daily sugar quota quite easily.

Lack of choice is never an excuse for skipping fruits and veggies. I used to opt out of eating veggie pizza, which I regularly made for others during my in-home cooking presentations. Then I had an amazingly simple epiphany. I could *choose* the toppings I liked and keep off the ones I didn't like when I made this for my family. Profound, I know. I didn't have to eat mushrooms (not a fan) or zucchini (not a fan). I could load up the crust with olives and peppers and broccoli and cauliflower and carrots with just a touch of red onion. My pizza. My favorites. My choice.

Fruits and vegetables are likely on your grocery list. They may even find their way into your shopping cart. Ideally, these items are the *first* to occupy your cart so that they leave less room for the not-as-good enticements that are to come. Often, though, we still derail ourselves. Far too often, cupcakes, cookies, and chips line the front entrance of our local grocery store right alongside the produce. Strategically placed "specials" with large signs offer discounted pricing. Superfans are encouraged to support their local team with enticing, decorated, baked creations. We're offered two-for-one deals on bags of chips in preparation for the weekend games or a national holiday.

If you're not confronted with temptation at the entrance, take a step farther inside the store. There, we often come face-to-face (or nose-to-nose) with the baked goods section, beckoning us closer and closer. Every whiff entices and whispers, "Try this. It can't hurt you." The battle is real. The marketing industry is on the prowl to deceive you.

Did you know that in some stores without bakeries, the store will pipe in the smell of one? For real. Research shows that when our sense of smell is stimulated, we will purchase more. According to the Scent Marketing Institute (yes, a real place like this exists), when the smell of fresh-baked bread was pumped into a grocery store, sales in the bakery department tripled.[2] A grocery chain in New York admittedly placed scent machines that released scents of chocolate and baking bread to make customers hungry and sales jumped.[3] The cards are stacked against us.

Even if we *do* make it past the enticements at the entrance, a stroll through the leafy greens is met with tempting options to make them more appealing . . . and less healthy. Crispy croutons, sugared nuts, sweetened dried fruits, and dressings offer to spice up bland greens. Our desire for sweet, sugary delight is stimulated. Temptation is everywhere.

By the time we navigate the store and, hopefully, make it past the yogurt aisle (I'll pray for those of you with toddlers), our willpower is often depleted. The ice cream and frozen pizza, or the predictable candy and goodies in the checkout line, end up in our cart, especially when shopping with kids. Our "no" muscle is simply worn out. Then, once the packaged foods are unloaded into our cabinets at home, we don't stand a chance. No matter how much willpower we have, those chips, cookies, or "snacks for the kids" *will* be eaten. By you. And me.

John Berardi is the cofounder of Precision Nutrition, the largest and most respected private nutrition coaching company in the world. His expertise is trusted by Apple, Equinox, Nike, and Titleist, and he was recently selected as one of the twenty smartest coaches in the world by Livestrong.com. He has shared this reality about our relationship with food:

> Berardi's First Law: If a food is in your possession or located in your residence, either you, someone you love, or someone you marginally tolerate will eventually eat it.[4]

If our goal is sustained or improved health, processed foods will not help us in our endeavors. If our shopping carts and kitchens are filled with less-than-nutritious foods every time we shop, we are in a constant fight with ourselves for control over our choices. We beat ourselves up, wear ourselves down, and just plain discourage ourselves from getting to where we truly want to be.

Did you know a lot of nutritionists eat mostly the same thing every day? Sound boring? Maybe even torturous? If you're someone who can enjoy variety while still making balanced, nutritious choices, go for it! Simplifying food choices has allowed me to stay more consistently on track with my health goals without having to count calories. This method does *not* mean sacrificing nutritional needs, however. It is crucial to include enough variety to meet the demands of your own body. Admittedly, it takes a bit of work through education and experimentation to find out what works for you.

Ultimately, you are the only one who is responsible for the daily decisions you make—whether it's what you eat, how you spend your time, or how you move your body. There are plenty of foods that will support your mind, body, and spirit, and other food counterfeits that simply will not. Some decisions take you closer to health and others drag you farther away. If you struggle with daily decisions, you are not alone. Rather than throwing in the towel at past failure, what if you bolstered your ability to make better decisions going forward?

Here are three ways to improve your decision-making ability:

Do the easy stuff first.
Make mornings a habit. Have a specific routine. Waking at the same time, knowing what you'll eat for breakfast, working out to a set schedule, and packing the same lunch before you head out the door reserves brainpower for the harder decisions the day will inevitably bring. Habits give our brains a break, prevent fatigue, and reserve willpower for when we really need it. Plus, starting our day in a healthy way is more likely to have a trickle-down impact on the rest of the decisions we make for the day that's ahead.

Anticipate the situation.
Much of our day is routine and mundane. When it isn't, however, our brains are taxed by having to choose. We can counteract this by having a preset plan. For example, if we know that our kid's demand for a ride to this friend's house or to that place to meet so-and-so may come the minute

he or she arrives home from school, have a predetermined response. Maybe it's deciding that on Tuesdays and Thursdays the answer is yes, and on the other days it's no. Or deciding not to have sleepovers on Saturday nights. When the request comes, and it will, the decision is automatic. If we are constantly at the beck and call of the next family "emergency" or work demand, we are more prone to make not-so-wise choices with our food and exercise.

Develop your habit muscle.

If you haven't read *The Power of Habit* by Charles Duhigg, put it on your must-read list. This book is the first step to changing our ability to make decisions. Habits free our brains so we can function on automatic pilot. Learn to leverage this ability to work *for* you. Things like brushing our teeth, reaching for a utensil in the kitchen, or shutting the garage door when we leave the house require no brainpower. They're instinctive. We can leverage this same power to develop behaviors around things like eating better, exercising more, or deepening our relationships. The stronger the muscle, the better the results.

If you're anything like me and you find decision-making daunting, these steps will help simplify and enhance your life. I've put these things into practice to reduce the number of times I'm faced with stressful situations. I'm a work in progress, just like you. I'm not an advocate of "perfect" food choices. I will never preach that a treat-free diet is the best way to live. All the foods before us, whether man-made or God-made, offer unique tasting experiences, many of which can be thoroughly enjoyed from time to time. Consider this wisdom from Voltaire:

Nothing would be more tiresome than eating and drinking if God had not made them a pleasure as well as a necessity.

When the bulk of our diets, however, are made up of processed foods that were made on a conveyer belt instead of grown in a garden, we are not making it easy to live a life of abundant health. When we choose preservatives over nutrients, we move further away from the food designed with our best interest in mind. We move further from God's best interest for us. Choose wisely.

*"That is why I tell you not to worry about
everyday life—whether you have enough food
and drink, or enough clothes to wear.
Isn't life more than food, and your body
more than clothing?"*
—Matthew 6:25

LESSON 3:

THE DEVIL'S NOT TO BLAME

As a customer service rep for a travel company (an entry-level, fresh-out-of-college job), I had my fill of complaint letters. A handful of those letters contained valid complaints. A delayed flight. A hotel in disrepair. Service that was nightmarish. But just as many were finger-wagging. Some to the point of absurdity. My favorites included:

- A customer demanding to be reimbursed for the money he lost at the airport slot machines in Vegas while waiting for his delayed flight.

- Another customer irate over the parking ticket a family member received when the pickup vehicle was left unattended in a no-parking zone at the airport due to the customer's delayed flight. He, too, demanded compensation.

They're not alone in their deflection of personal responsibility. The US Chamber Institute for Legal Reform compiles a list of the top-ten most frivolous lawsuits each year. Included recently were:

- A bank robber who sued the county for $6.3 million to cover medical expenses after he received a pair of slugs while fleeing a police officer.

- A twelve-year-old boy who was sued by his aunt for a "careless" hug when he was eight that caused her to fall and break her wrist. She demanded $127,000, claiming the boy "should have known that a forceful greeting such as the one delivered by the defendant to the plaintiff could cause the harm and losses suffered by the plaintiff."

- A female student who sued her college, saying "anxiety and depression made it difficult for her to concentrate" and her "professor didn't do enough to help her pass a class on adult health patterns."[5]

We laugh. Ridiculous, right? Yet, are we really any different? We love wagging our fingers. We love making an excuse for a choice that didn't work out so well. We don't like taking responsibility when bad stuff happens to us.

Look at our heritage. Adam and Eve may be the only two people in history who could have legitimately cast blame on a very culpable opponent, but was the serpent really to blame? Let's revisit the story.

> *The serpent was the shrewdest of all the wild animals the Lord God had made. One day he asked the woman, "Did God really say you must not eat the fruit from any of the trees in the garden?"*
>
> *"Of course we may eat fruit from the trees in the garden," the woman replied. "It's only the fruit from the tree in the middle of the garden that*

we are not allowed to eat. God said, 'You must not eat it or even touch it; if you do, you will die.'"

"You won't die!" the serpent replied to the woman. "God knows that your eyes will be opened as soon as you eat it, and you will be like God, knowing both good and evil."

The woman was convinced. She saw that the tree was beautiful and its fruit looked delicious, and she wanted the wisdom it would give her. So she took some of the fruit and ate it. Then she gave some to her husband, who was with her, and he ate it, too. (Genesis 3:1–6)

Did you catch it? It's subtle. Eve *wanted* the wisdom it would give her. She *desired* it. The serpent was just the catalyst. The trigger.

Dr. Ed Young is an author and senior pastor of Fellowship Church, a multisite church based in Houston, Texas. Dr. Young has valued physical and spiritual fitness so strongly in his career that his church has an exercise club and gym on its primary campus. He describes Satan's subtle approach this way:

> [Satan] knows you're too smart to fall for the temptation to jump off a bridge, throw yourself in front of a speeding train, or drink a bottle of cyanide . . . Remember: he's a con artist. He wants to trick you into doing his bidding, to cause you to think it's not too bad. So he just might suggest more acceptable behaviors that could eventually gain him the same result, behaviors that will negatively affect your health.[6]

Have you met desire face-to-face yet? Has the serpent whispered to you? I bet he has. Maybe he's the chips in the pantry. The candy dish in the office. The popcorn in the movie theater (not that I'd know anything about that). Insert your subtle or not-so-subtle temptation. Your desire. It's there, even if you try to ignore it.

Eve gave in to subtlety. She didn't need much prompting or coercing. It was her *own* desire that led her into temptation. It didn't feel like bridge-jumping. Rather than recognizing this and acknowledging the truth, however, she wagged her finger in response to Adam's accusation:

> *"Have you eaten from the tree whose fruit I commanded you not to eat?"*
>
> *The man replied, "It was the woman you gave me who gave me the fruit, and I ate it."*
>
> *Then the Lord God asked the woman, "What have you done?"*
>
> *"The serpent deceived me," she replied. "That's why I ate it."* (Genesis 3:11–13)

Adam blamed Eve, and ultimately, God, for putting her there. In self-defense, Eve pointed her finger directly at the serpent. Both looked for scapegoats, reasons for their inability to resist temptation. They wanted to be reimbursed.

In psychology, the term used for the belief system that creates this behavior is "external locus of control." Essentially, this is believing that outside influences are the primary reason for the result. When something good (or bad) happens, you instinctively point to luck, fate, timing, other people, divine intervention . . . or serpents . . . as the cause.

In contrast, having an "internal locus of control" means feeling personally responsible for the outcome. When something good (or bad) happens, you attribute your own actions to the success or failure.

Adam and Eve were external-locus-of-control kind of people. They were the first to identify the serpent as the reason for their lack of personal control and, therefore, shortfall. They wrote a letter to customer service and demanded compensation. They searched through the Yellow Pages or Google looking for an attorney. Yet there was no justifiable finger-pointing. Yes, the serpent planted the seed, but he simply fed what he *knew* was at the core of these first humans. He knew their weakness because he had it, too, and he exploited it. He also knows mine, and he knows yours. It hasn't changed.

> *Temptation comes from our own desires, which entice us and drag us away. These desires give birth to sinful actions. And when sin is allowed to grow, it gives birth to death.* (James 1:14–15)

It's our own desires, our hearts, our longings, our wants, our wishes, and our cravings. No one causes us to sin. No one forces us into temptation. We are hardwired with desires that lead us away from truth, light, and the life God intended for us to lead—a life that's abundant instead of diseased.

The apostle Paul understood. One of the most God-loving, Christ-exemplifying men in the Bible (after his dramatic conversion) fought his own personal battle with desire. He understood and struggled with it.

> *I don't really understand myself, for I want to do what is right, but I don't do it. Instead, I do what I hate.* (Romans 7:15)

Temptation is hard, and it's personal. What's yours? It might be the desire to drive by the gym instead of stopping after work as planned. It might be hitting the

Snooze button instead of getting out of bed for that early morning workout. Maybe it's going out with friends after work for one drink, only to find yourself indulging in one too many. Or it could be that movie popcorn you'd decided you wouldn't have until you smelled it (again, no personal experience here).

We find all kinds of ways to justify our decisions. Work was brutal. You were called on to play taxi for your kids. You were up late and needed the extra sleep. You think you feel a cold coming on. It's cold outside. You don't like vegetables. The pantry is nearly bare. The dog ate your last chicken breast—and your homework . . . have I hit yours yet?

Excuses. Blame. Whatever you want to call it. It's putting responsibility somewhere else. Remember that external locus of control? We point our fingers at something other than ourselves, something beyond our control, and it makes us feel better. We do it so well.

Like most preteen girls, I was acutely aware of my body and the changes that were happening in early middle school. I knew my mom and sister were *not* built like me. They were smaller, and I didn't like it. At all. I remember the day I stood in front of my full-length bathroom mirror and saw, and felt, my thighs touch for the first time. Though these "thunder thighs" would serve me well as a high school and college athlete, they were my greatest point of self-consciousness. I blamed faulty genetics.

I carried this finger-pointing into adulthood. My pregnancies brought big babies and huge weight gain. I added over fifty pounds to my five-foot-four-inch frame with my firstborn, Drew. After he arrived at ten pounds one ounce (ouch), I expected the weight to fall off, but seven months later and pregnant with baby number two, I'd lost only a small fraction of the weight. I blamed my husband.

Alex weighed in at nine pounds twelve ounces (again, ouch), and I hovered above a healthy weight for the next year. I blamed young children, lack of sleep, a colicky baby, and anything that walked, moved, or breathed.

I finally shed the extra pounds with dietary changes and exercise but four years later regained them with my third pregnancy at age thirty-two. Kyle arrived at less than nine pounds . . . by half an ounce. Though I rebounded from his birth more quickly, I still found room for finger-wagging. I blamed the arrival of varicose veins, deepening stretch marks, and increasingly saggy body parts on this final pregnancy.

At age thirty-four, I was just starting to enjoy running for the first time in my life and had half marathons in my sight. But my knee had other plans. I wasn't surprised since my high school and college years were spent catching fast-pitch, double-header softball games and digging balls on the volleyball court. But it forced me to stop running. Cue the finger-wagging. I blamed my past.

After a year of medical appointments, diagnostic testing, and treatments, it was clear that running would not be in my future. As a result, my weight began to steadily climb during this hiatus from the treadmill, and I was discouraged and frustrated. Swimming left me cold (literally), biking left me sore (need I say more?), and the elliptical was just plain boring. I tried a variety of group classes, too, but I wasn't seeing the results I desired. I was heavy and discouraged. I blamed my bum knee.

Sitting on my couch at age thirty-eight, I saw an infomercial that changed the trajectory of my life (though I didn't know it at the time). I was sick and tired of being sick and tired. It was time to do *something*. I was tired of blame.

Have you been there? Have you had that moment yet? Maybe it was a photograph or the avoidance of it because it might appear on social media. Maybe you were tired of tucking yourself in the back row of family pictures, hoping you could hide from a full-body shot.

Or maybe you were strategically cropping a picture to hide your imperfections. Maybe it was a special occasion you skipped because you were embarrassed to be seen. Maybe it was a bad report at the doctor's office and fear of where it might lead. Or maybe it was a medical emergency for you or a family member that made you realize it was a preventable disease. What did you blame? Are you still wagging your finger today?

In 2009, at age thirty-eight, I stopped blaming my health, and my body, on something or somebody else. It was my choice, my responsibility. In a rare, non-deliberative moment, I ordered the workout program from that infomercial. I didn't have a lot to lose (except weight), and I did have a whole lot to gain (my health back). For extra accountability, I recruited my husband, Kevin, to do the program with me. After ninety days, we experienced the benefits of that choice. We lost weight, got stronger, and started eating better. It kick-started what was to become a lifestyle for us and a career specialization for me, but it only happened when I was ready to stop wagging my finger. I had to shelve blame.

Life is filled with moments of choice like this one. To blame or not to blame. When life changes, it's just another opportunity to adjust, to choose fresh, to choose new. The fight doesn't stop at age thirty, forty, fifty, or sixty plus. Each decade (each year?) brings change. Our bodies change. We process food differently, burn fat differently, store fat differently, and respond to stress differently. Hormones ebb and flow with each decade. There is a constant need to be creative with exercise, food intake, and the choices we make in our day-to-day lives.

Often, we blame a plateau for our decision to stop trying. In truth, plateaus are simply our bodies' way of letting us know it's time to change again—to move and eat differently, to learn more, to adjust. They're a signal that something has changed with how we're eating, drinking, or moving or how our hormones are functioning. It's our job to do some digging to figure out what's changed and why and, most importantly, to decide what to do about it. Sometimes, it's okay to accept the changes and be content with our bodies just as they are. Our bodies are made to change with time. Other times, we may need to adjust something for the sake of our health. Whatever decision we make is 100 percent up to us.

I know it's hard to feel at war with your body and with food and exercise. It truly is a war. The same culprit who was at work in the Garden is still at work today.

> *Stay alert! Watch out for your great enemy, the devil. He prowls around like a roaring lion, looking for someone to devour.* (1 Peter 5:8)

Wow. That's sobering. We are fighting the same fight Adam and Eve first battled in the Garden and that every generation, every person, has fought since, thousands of years later. Now, instead of a tantalizing piece of fruit (imagine if *that* were our greatest temptation!), it's something that comes in a box or a package. It's a store-bought treat or fast-food meal that speaks to our desire. It's a man-made food instead of a God-made food.

What if you pictured your great enemy, Satan, lurking behind the counter of your favorite fast-food restaurant offering you a supersized meal? What if you heard him roar with delight with every sip of that soda or bite of that doughnut? What if he hovered around the vending machine ready to devour you after you push B3? Would that change your choice?

A bit dramatic? Maybe, but are the consequences of our decisions really that much different from what they were for Adam and Eve? God promised death with a *single* bite of that fruit. Though it may take more than one bite of a pastry or one sip of a sugary soft drink, add up a lifetime of single bites and the outcome is the same. Yes, everyone will face death eventually—that's inevitable—but we can improve the quality of today and tomorrow with more nourishing single-bite choices.

What kind of desire is leading you away from the life you always wanted? What do you need to say *no* to so you can say *yes* to a better, healthier tomorrow?

Here are three ways you can accept responsibility and take action today:

Adopt one new habit.

Choose *one* thing to change today. Use the addition principle. Add rather than subtract. Add a good-for-you food into your life rather than taking something away. For example, add a glass of water, a vegetable, or a piece of fruit each day rather than taking away dessert, soda, or bread. Let's approach this from the perspective of healthy additions rather than deprivations. You are much more likely to see long-term success with this method. The residual choice of adding things in is watching the other things naturally take a back seat in your day-to-day diet. Test me and try to prove me wrong!

Don't be an overachiever.

Promise me you'll stick with only *one habit change* at a time. I know some of you ambitious overachiever types will want to do it all at once. I get it! I'm a recovering perfectionist. But what happened the last time you decided to "get healthy?" More than likely, you tried to change a lot of things at once. One oft-cited personal experiment showed that your success rate is 80 percent when you change one thing at a time. Add two changes, and success drops to under 35 percent. Three changes result in a measly 5 percent success rate.[7] I want you to succeed! Even if it's slower than you'd like, the results will be far more sustainable and rewarding. Be a tortoise, not a hare.

Shape the path.

Set up your environment for success. Ideally, keep tempting foods out of your home. I know this can be a tough battle to fight when you have kids, but establishing healthy eating choices early on is the best way you can shape their future relationship with food. Put more fruits and veggies at eye level in the fridge so they're the first thing everyone sees when opening the doors. If you *do* have "kid snacks" in the house and they're the first thing you see when you open the pantry, shove them to the back if you can't get rid of them. Similarly, shape your path to exercise by removing temptations to skip it. If the sofa or favorite chair calls to you when you walk in the door, put some hand weights on your favorite cushion so you'll be reminded to *use* them!

Adam and Eve gave in to their desires. They were tempted by what they wanted but couldn't have. They pointed their perfectly crafted fingers beyond themselves and deflected responsibility. You can choose differently and take responsibility for your choices. For the good of your health—and life—stop wagging your finger.

People who conceal their sins will not prosper,
but if they confess and turn from them,
they will receive mercy.
—Proverbs 28:13

LESSON 4:

FIG-LEAF JACKETS ARE HOLEY

Do you remember the first time you felt shame? You probably do. Once you experience that powerful emotion for the first time, it's hardwired into you. My own memory is crystal clear, and, though it happened in childhood, it's still not something I'm willing to share on these pages. That's the power of shame. It's personal, private, and painful.

Shame is very different from guilt, though they often get lumped together. Guilt is about what we *did* . . . our behavior. Shame is about who we *are* . . . our character. Guilt is temporary. Shame is longer lasting, even permanent. Shame makes us cover ourselves up and hide. We want to become invisible—like Adam and Eve. They ate the fruit and came face-to-face with each other and with shame.

> *The woman was convinced. She saw that the tree was beautiful and its fruit looked delicious, and she wanted the wisdom it would give her. So she took some of the fruit and ate it. Then she gave some to her husband, who was with her, and he ate it, too. At that moment, their eyes were opened, and they suddenly felt shame at their nakedness. So they sewed fig leaves together to cover themselves.* (Genesis 3:6–7)

The early onset of body image issues. Why do you think their nakedness was the first thing they noticed? And why was it so shameful? Do you think they felt more than just their physical nakedness? I think so. I think it was the whole-life kind of exposure—totally stripped bare, completely vulnerable with eyes wide open to all they couldn't see before. Maybe they realized the serpent was right in a twisted way.

They received wisdom, all right, but it wasn't the wisdom they anticipated. Instead, it was recognition of just how far they were from the one and only perfect God and just how far they'd now fallen. The reflection they saw in each other was nothing like the image they saw of their Maker, and they didn't like it. Adam and Eve were perfectly created in the image of God. Wonderfully made.

> So God created human beings in his own image.
> In the image of God he created them; male and
> female he created them. (Genesis 1:27)

It was the perfect blueprint, each one distinct yet completing a perfect likeness and perfect whole together. Together, they were one. They should have seen this perfection in each other and how complementary they were. And they did. (Remember the "felt no shame" part?)

Yet post-apple, they saw distortion. They felt the need to grab a few fig leaves and cover themselves up. They created fig-leaf jackets. But despite the coverings, they were still exposed. The jackets were holey, and God still saw them.

> When the cool evening breezes were blowing,
> the man and his wife heard the Lord God walking
> about in the garden. So they hid from the Lord
> God among the trees.

Then the Lord God called to the man, "Where are you?"

He replied, "I heard you walking in the garden, so I hid. I was afraid because I was naked."

"Who told you that you were naked?" the Lord God asked. "Have you eaten from the tree whose fruit I commanded you not to eat?" (Genesis 3:8–11)

Their instinct was to hide, to cover themselves with the only thing they thought would suitably cover their private parts—big ol' leaves. Then they hid the rest of themselves in the shadows of the trees.

My middle son, Alex, had a high school classmate, "Charlie," who was caught at an underage drinking party. As the cops approached the house and the kids dispersed, Charlie ran and hid behind a tree with a trunk far too narrow to conceal him. The cop saw him, cuffed him, and escorted him to the squad car. After he was securely in custody, the cop jumped behind a tree himself and said tauntingly, "Can you see me?" It's kind of a funny picture unless you're the one trying to hide behind the tree.

Charlie lost his opportunity to play with his team in the soccer playoffs his senior year, a team on which he was a captain. I don't know if he fessed up or apologized. It didn't matter; the consequences stuck.

I don't think God was taunting Adam and Eve. He knew exactly what they'd done, and he could see them, hiding behind a tree that was far too narrow to conceal them no matter how massive its trunk. Even the giant fig leaves were far too small to help their cause. He saw them completely and gave them an opportunity to confess. They had the chance to acknowledge their not-so-great choice and take responsibility for it, but we know the choice they made. They didn't.

I wonder what God would have done if Adam and Eve had apologized and asked for forgiveness. Would they still have gotten the judgment they did? Very likely, since a good and fair God must act on the promises he makes, even when it brings him personal pain. He warns us, clarifies the consequences, and then lets us choose. Sometimes he gives us more than one chance. Sometimes he doesn't. Adam and Eve made their choice. As a result, shame gripped them ferociously, and they retreated to their hiding place. Though they felt adequately concealed, their shame blinded them to the gaping holes in their fig-leaf jackets. Their patch job couldn't fully hide their nakedness. Their jackets were holey.

How holey is yours? What are you trying to conceal? Maybe it's a hidden behavior or relationship like the ones my clients reveal to me. As tears well in their eyes or slide down their cheeks, these brave souls cautiously lift one corner of their jackets, remove one little leaf, and show me a glimpse of what lies underneath, things they've kept hidden for years and never told anyone.

Like "Karen," who can't escape the grocery store without binging on cookies, baked goods, or other treats, tossing whatever remains in the package before leaving the store. Her husband knows nothing about this behavior, nor do her closest friends. She feels powerless over this compulsion. Shame.

Or "Sally," whose long-term secret relationship with another woman was completely hidden for over thirty years until this silent partner's death. At the time of her passing, the relationship was still a secret, even to the other woman's children. This relationship kept Sally isolated from anybody and everybody for her entire adult life, and she's still trying to pick up the pieces. Shame.

Maybe, for you, it's an obsession with body image. The constant pursuit of the ideal shape and weight leaves you perpetually dissatisfied with the way you look. Or waging a secret battle with disordered eating, like "Holly," whose background as a teen model led to a full-blown eating disorder. As an adult today, her addiction manifests itself in excess alcohol consumption and an ongoing battle to control her binge desires for food. Shame.

Maybe your body issues are even more personal, a private shame that's the result of physical abuse, neglect, or sexual promiscuity, the consequences of things done in private, in the dark, that have left deep scars whether inflicted by yourself or others. These are far more than just vanity issues. These are deeper and darker. This kind of shame is painfully personal and private. It's often not shared with anyone for fear of how others will see you or judge you. Maybe your deepest fear is that others will see right through you to your nakedness, peeping through what feels like big, gaping holes in your fig-leaf jacket, even when you've done your best to bury yourself in the leaves. Despite trying to hide from yourself and everyone else, you still feel vulnerable and exposed.

Maybe, instead of a jacket, you're wearing a fig-leaf blanket, quilted over years and years of hiding—an immersive covering you've hand sewn one leafy square at a time, a patchwork history of one shameful experience after another until your entire life feels covered and protected. The truth is, no matter how protected you think you are, eventually, someone will find you. Someone will lift an edge or peek through a seam. Someone will want to see you and know you, just like God did with Adam and Eve.

The original inhabitants of Earth's first garden feared what God would see in their nakedness. They didn't have time to make a blanket. This was their first offense, their introduction to shame. So they grabbed some leaves and hid. The fig-leaf jacket weaving had begun.

We do the same thing. We run from God instead of toward him. We are quick to believe we have disappointed him in some way, and we don't want to talk about it. We hide in the tree's shadows with our barely there fig leaves, hoping we won't be found or stripped of our protection. Sadly, this also puts us that much further from what God truly wants for us. He wants us to say, "I'm sorry," while running into his all-encompassing Daddy arms so he can love us and forgive us. He wants to heal us and forgive us, and it's always available, always, just as it was to Adam and Eve.

No matter what you've done, or what life has done to you, it's never too late to run into those arms, but to get there means removing the fig leaves one at a time.

Leaf one. Anger.
Leaf two. Pain.
Leaf three. Silence.
Leaf four. Judgment.
Leaf five. Shame.

With each stripped leaf, we get closer and closer to who we are truly created to be—stripped and naked but somehow freer. We shed the deepest-of-Minnesota-winter parka and replace it with a Hawaiian Islands tank top. Lighter and freer.

Even those who aren't harboring deep, gut-wrenching shame could likely use some leaf blowing. It's time to drop the leaves that have distorted our view of ourselves and our bodies, the ones that clamor for our attention and create a fixation with all that is wrong with our bodies instead of all that's amazing about them. If you aren't sure whether you struggle with body image, the next two words will help you decide. Swimsuit shopping. I'm pretty sure I just heard you groan.

My friend "Bethany" ventured semi-enthusiastically

into this treacherous territory after diligently following an intense exercise program for ten weeks. She expected to notice changes, but instead, she landed in an all-too-familiar place: her expectations didn't match the reflection in the mirror.

In *Sports Illustrated*'s infamous swimsuit issue, perfectly sculpted bodies envelop page after page of the magazine. With today's technology, we know these perfect bodies are the result of airbrushing and, often, extreme dieting. Yet, if we're honest, there's a teeny-tiny part of us that, way down deep, believes that *maybe*, with enough hard work, we might achieve that ideal shape or at least *some* kind of shape.

As women, we constantly fight body image issues. Remember the thunder thighs I discovered in that bathroom mirror as a middle-school girl? Even today, when I stand and look in a dressing room mirror, my eyes instinctively target my legs, especially when swimsuit shopping. I have a long mental list of body imperfections—veins, cellulite, stretch marks, wrinkles, gray hair, and sagging skin to name a few. But to this day, my thighs remain my biggest nemesis. I'm probably in better physical condition than I was as a college athlete twenty-five years ago. I've been a size 14+ and a size 2. Yet, regardless of size and shape, I find fault. I know I am "fearfully and wonderfully made" (Psalms 139:14). I know my "inner self and gentle spirit" is of greatest worth to God (1 Peter 3:4). Yet I can still doubt these truths.

Let's prioritize God's primary commandment:

> *Jesus replied, "You must love the Lord your God with all your heart, all your soul, and all your mind. This is the first and greatest commandment. A second is equally important: Love your neighbor as yourself."* (Matthew 22:37-39)

Wait. Did you catch that? Love *yourself*. Self-love is *assumed*. It's *expected*. Whoa. It's expected not just when we have the perfect body, not just when we can stand contentedly in a dressing room, but *all* the time—size 2 or size 14+.

In the privacy of her own home, Bethany modeled a few swimsuit contenders for her husband (sharing none of her personal narrative about her body or the suits). He showered her with positive and encouraging words. He saw what she didn't. He loved her just as she was. He saw inside the fig leaves. She kept *two* of the suits.

God is our clearest mirror. He offers us the best reflection of who we really are, without distortion or filters. He sees beyond our "trouble spots" and our fixations to the core of who we truly are. When our judgment is skewed and shame clouds our perceptions, it is he who offers his unbiased opinion and showers us with the positive and encouraging words we are unable to say to ourselves. God created us in his image, and he sees the beauty. So if we were created in his likeness and desire to see what he sees, we need to know what it means to be in his image. If we look solely at Jesus's physical features, we've got our eyes fixed on the wrong thing.

The Bible is nearly silent about Jesus's physical appearance. We get our only glimpse in the book of Isaiah:

> *My servant grew up in the Lord's presence like a tender green shoot, like a root in dry ground. There was nothing beautiful or majestic about his appearance, nothing to attract us to him.*
> (Isaiah 53:2)

Interesting. There was nothing stunning about Jesus. We would likely have walked by him on the street. His followers were not drawn to him because of his good looks. He was unremarkable in stature. He was not a movie star on the red carpet. He was no Jim Caviezel or Christian Bale (both of whom portrayed Jesus on the big screen). The blue-eyed, blond-haired, gleaming portrait we see so often in our attempts to represent him are likely not accurate at all. We've photoshopped Jesus.

Our humanity beautifies him. We expect that if he's perfect, it carries over to our human view of our outward appearance as well. But the Bible's pretty clear that Jesus wasn't visually perfect. He doesn't expect us to be either, and he certainly never intended to use our bodies as a source of shame.

Can we truly love ourselves just as we are? Can we call a truce with our bodies?

Here are three things you can do today to release the shame you carry:

Take off your running shoes.

No matter how hard or how fast you run, God will find you. You can't outrun the God who loves you. If you're trying to escape your past with food, exercise, alcohol, or promiscuity, let me ask you this: How's that working for you? Trying to outrun your past, or present, will not lead you to a better road in the future. It's time to slow down. It's hard. I get it. We are our own worst critics. We barrage ourselves with negative self-talk that we hear more clearly when we stop long enough to listen. But becoming aware that your life isn't working in this state of shame is the first step to slowing your run to a walk. Eventually, you'll learn to be still; for now, just slow your pace.

Start a mulching business.

Those fig leaves need to go. You don't have to start with the biggest leaf; a tiny one will do. Maybe it means telling a trusted friend. Maybe it means starting a journal to document your feelings and to begin to release the secret thoughts that haunt you. Or, if you're ready to release it, get in touch with a great counselor who can help you process and acknowledge the challenges you are facing. Your past doesn't have to define your future. Shame can't survive in the light.

Wave the white flag.

Surrender to the God who's given you a new line of clothes. God took your fig leaves, all of them, and wore them all the way to a tree that was waiting to receive him. He took each leaf and placed it strategically on his own broken and beaten body so that we would no longer have to be fig-leaf wearers. He's waiting for you to accept that truth and live in that truth. We dishonor him by choosing to wear those leaves again when he gave his life to take them from us. He's forgiven you. Have you forgiven yourself?

Are you ready? Stop running. Start mulching. And surrender. Strip and shed the fig leaves that are covering your life. Thy swimsuit self needs you.

Thank you for making me so wonderfully
complex! Your workmanship is marvelous—
how well I know it.
—Psalms 139:14

GOD WILL GIVE YOU MORE THAN YOU CAN HANDLE

"Debbie's" husband abandoned her. He brainwashed her young daughters into disowning her as well. She spent two years barely eating, rarely leaving the couch, and only surviving thanks to the love of a friend.

"Fiona" survived what should have been a life-ending neck break (the worst kind) after a car accident as a teenager. After living in a halo for months, she was subsequently diagnosed with thyroid cancer. She beat the cancer, but now eats fewer than seven hundred calories a day due to swallowing challenges from the accident and a paralyzing fear of vomiting.

"Laurie" is the primary caregiver for her terminally ill husband in addition to working a full-time corporate job. She lost over thirty pounds but regained it with the stress of the day-to-day grind and the not-so-subtle sabotage efforts from her husband.

"Jaqueline" lost her husband to cancer. "Rachel's" husband left her . . . while she was eight months pregnant. "Tony" was molested as a teenager.

These are just a few of the real-life stories I've collected over the years. If you heard firsthand the pain and brokenness in their words and saw the tears that flowed, you'd likely agree that they were given far more than any one person could handle. The pain was crushing.

One often-used phrase that originated from an errant interpretation of a Bible verse is "God won't give you more than you can handle." In difficult times, this phrase is spouted by well-meaning, well-intentioned people who are trying to encourage someone. Maybe you've used it. I know I have. The intention is good. The interpretation is wrong. The misquoted verse comes from 1 Corinthians, which reads:

> *The temptations in your life are no different from what others experience. And God is faithful. He will not allow the temptation to be more than you can stand. When you are tempted, he will show you a way out so that you can endure.*
> (1 Corinthians 10:13)

Notice the difference. We are *not* told we won't encounter more than we can handle; we are promised that we won't be *tempted* beyond what we can stand. This makes all the difference in how we approach challenges. I believe this verse holds more hope than our inaccurate interpretation. There are promises held deeply in these verses.

Promise #1. We *all* face temptation. It's not a matter of if; it's a matter of when. We can and should expect it. Admittedly, that's maybe not the kind of promise we want to hear. We'd rather avoid temptation altogether. But this human experience is one we all share. Though your challenge likely looks different from mine, the feeling of, and encounter with, temptation is universal. There's a uniqueness, yet a commonality, to the experience.

Why does this matter? Because we can encourage one another. We get it. We've been there. Not only can we console one another but we're expected to do so—commanded to, more accurately.

> *So encourage each other and build each other up,*
> *just as you are already doing.* (1 Thessalonians 5:11)

We have built-in partners, others who can help us and relate to us. This includes people who have gone before us and navigated through temptation well. It also includes those who haven't done so well and who have learned valuable lessons from their journeys. We learn from successes and failures.

Adam and Eve didn't have this. There were no friends or family to help them work through their decision, no one to say, "Yep, I think the snake's right. Go for it!" Or, "No way, José! He's a loser. Flee!" I guess that was one of the challenges of being first—no fleshy friends. But, unlike us, they had personal, direct communication with their Creator. They had it from the ultimate authority that the snake had it all wrong. It was a firsthand message delivery system with crystal clarity.

Christ's empathy led him to, later in the story, endure his own temptation on multiple occasions while walking the earth as God in the flesh so that he could uniquely relate to us. He withstood more opportunities to turn his back on his Father than we ever will. His impending death on the cross gave him ample opportunity to justify giving in to *his* desire to remove himself from the kind of suffering God promised him.

Honestly, we probably would have understood if he had turned his back on his mission and fled. He would have been justified to wag his finger at his accusers and say, "I did nothing wrong. I'm innocent. All these other people in the room and the others who are walking around this earth? They're the ones to blame. And don't even get me started on the ones that are to come. They're why I'm here, because they are going to make so many mistakes. So just forget it. This is way too hard and so not fair. I'm leaving." He could have returned to his throne unscathed, yet he chose endurance.

Jesus was fully human in every way. He relates to our enticements, whether it's the draw of alcohol, the overindulgence at a meal, or the attractiveness of another person. He was offered opportunities to compromise, but he chose a better path. Why? Because Jesus understood his purpose and God's plan. This single-minded focus allowed him to say no to temptation. He saw that the end game was greater than any temporary pleasure in the moment. He knew God's ideal for his life, and he chose to pursue it passionately. This meant forgoing the temporary for the eternal.

His pain and suffering were far more than we could ever endure or imagine, but he chose that path because it was God's path—a path that led to life for you and for me.

Promise #2. We can endure, too. God has equipped us to be strong and to stand against the challenges we face. We are powerful! God designed us that way, in his image.

> For God has not given us a spirit of fear and timidity, but of power, love, and self-discipline. (2 Timothy 1:7)

We have the strength to withstand. We can be powerful, loving, and even self-disciplined. Yes, it's easier to give in. It's easier to stop fighting when we're exhausted after a long day. The fast-food drive-through is a quick solution when we haven't planned or prepared our dinner for that night. A Big Mac, large fries, and Diet Coke promise happiness, sustenance, and instant hunger management. Why drive by when we can drive through?

Yet this behavior won't lead us to a healthy future. The instant gratification is outweighed by the insulin spike, blood sugar crash, and energy depletion that ensues shortly after ingesting that fast-food meal. We set ourselves up for, and experience, the exact opposite impact of what we crave—nourishment, satiety, and energy.

Additionally, we set failure in motion by developing a pattern—or habit—of driving through that restaurant for relief each time we're stressed, tired, or famished. The habit loop begins with a cue (seeing the restaurant), followed by a routine (driving through), and ending in a reward (instant gratification). In this case, the "reward" doesn't lead us to our long-term goal, like weight loss, but takes us further from it. We sabotage ourselves by establishing a reward system that's not so rewarding. Self-discipline is a part of our innermost being. It's at our core, in our being. We just have to tap into it. But that, admittedly, is not easy. Sometimes, we feel depleted and exhausted. Temptation threatens to engulf us. That leads to the next promise.

Promise #3. Even when *we* are not strong, God *is*. He will show you a way out, another option. But how often do we ask for help? How often do we choose prayer in times of temptation? We may, when the temptation feels big and hairy; if we are faced with what feels like a seemingly monumental hurdle or overwhelming obstacle, we often shoot up a "help me" prayer.

But how about in day-to-day, smaller battles? Do we pray when we need help walking past the grocery store's bakery? Do we ask for help when we see the Girl Scouts lined up outside the neighborhood store peddling their cookies? How about when we work from our home office, which also happens to be our kitchen, and the freshly baked chocolate chip cookies are staring at us from the counter? (Not that I know about that.)

I know I am guilty of relying on my *own* strength, my *own* willpower, my *own* self-discipline. Though we are encouraged to be strong and brave, we are also reminded that we have a constant companion with us. Always. We can't do it on our strength alone; we need God to intervene and interrupt our cyclical patterns—the ones that scream, "Me, me, me!" When we allow God to work in our lives, the result will be a recognition that *he* did it, not me. We remind ourselves, and others, that there is a God and he gets the glory.

> *This is my command—be strong and coura-geous! Do not be afraid or discouraged. For the Lord your God is with you wherever you go.* (Joshua 1:9)

It's easier to remember this in the big stuff, when something significant is on the line and we need God's help, but it's easy to forget when we're facing those smaller struggles with temptation. Sometimes we let our impatience, fatigue, or apathy get the best of us. God provides an out—a solution—to the big temptations and the little ones.

Promise #4. God is faithful, even when we screw up—and we will. Sometimes we just can't help ourselves. Like Eve. And Mac.

Mac is our family's Cavalier King Charles spaniel. Known for their intelligence, obedience, and docile nature, they are the perfect family pet . . . if you like dogs. Since Cavaliers were originally bred as hunting dogs, their instinct is to chase. It's their nature. They beeline for their "prey" without recognizing danger in their periphery. Being warned of this when we chose this breed and realizing we couldn't protect him all the time, we had an invisible fence installed in our backyard and included professional training classes.

During the training period, a perimeter of flags was established around the yard. As Mac approached a flag, a sound chirped from his collar. A warning. When he got too close, however, he'd get a small shock, which left him shaking his head while retreating. The trainer had four primary jobs: relate, teach, tempt, reward.

Relating was first. Nothing would be accomplished until the relationship was established. She had to get to know Mac's personality and gain his trust. She'd throw toys, run with him all over the backyard, and give him lots of praise.

Teaching came next. It began by wiggling an established flag and saying "No" to Mac. She set the boundary. She taught him the flags were to be minded, and she warned him of the looming danger.

Then she tempted. It was the longest phase. A desired toy, something that was nearly irresistible for a puppy, was thrown beyond the boundary. In the beginning, Mac didn't hesitate. He'd race for it every time. He ignored the warning signal and suffered the shocking consequences. After a few rounds, however, Mac started to catch on. He started to hesitate. He'd make his way more slowly toward the desired object—that perfectly shaped, fun-colored sphere. (Sound familiar?) Sometimes he'd heed the warning sound and stop. Other times, he just couldn't help it. The temptation was too great. His desire was too strong.

Reward only came when, and if, he bypassed temptation. When earned, it came quickly and heartily. The trainer joyfully praised Mac and rewarded his obedience with a tasty treat. It was his compensation for not chasing the object that lay beyond the established boundary, the inside-the-boundaries reward that was freely given because of obedience. The trainer was faithful.

She readily and willingly gave from her bag of goodies while encouraging Mac with words of affirmation and a load of attention.

"Good boy, Mac!"

"Well done!" (my good and faithful servant)

The ear scratching alone may have been enough to keep him in bounds, but alongside it was the promised reward and praise. Bonus! Eventually, the backyard boundary flags were removed one by one as Mac earned the trust of his trainer. They became unnecessary. Mac didn't even need the instantly gratifying treat to obey the rules. He just needed endorsement from his owners, the ones who loved him, of a job well done. He learned to avoid temptation, not just to avoid pain but because he received something much better if he said no. He found joy in obedience.

That doesn't mean he's perfect. On occasion, Mac slips up. His canine training extended to parts inside the house as well. There are spaces that are off limits. Kenzie, our cat, knows this and finds it amusing to mercilessly taunt him by staying just out of his reach. Sometimes, when they're tussling, Mac just can't control himself. He puts one paw (or two . . . or four) into the forbidden space to gain the extra inches he needs to reach Kenzie, who then retreats farther. We really could have called her Satan.

Or sometimes, in his energetic play, a toy ends up beyond the boundary. If no one's looking, he'll be across and back so quickly to retrieve it that we don't have time to scold him. Mac knows we love him (though I'm more of a cat person). He is fed, groomed, walked, played with, and praised. We are faithful. He is faithful back.

How much greater, then, is God's faithfulness? Unlike Mac, Adam and Eve didn't have to earn it. They had it from day one. He was a natural relator. As Teacher, God showed them all the goodness inside the Garden. There was so much to be experienced. There were colors to be enjoyed, relationships to be developed, flavors to be tasted, and spaces to run and roam. God held nothing good back from them, but he knew their instinct. He wanted to protect them. He wiggled the apple (at least that's the way I picture it) to make it clear what was to be avoided, and said, "No." He did so not because he was withholding but because he knew the danger. God knew their nature, the peripheral blind spots they couldn't see when they were singularly focused on the chase. Their desire.

Maybe God should have built in a warning signal. A little chirping sound around that apple. Or maybe he did. I think he's named the Holy Spirit. Maybe Eve hesitated. Maybe she heard that little warning sound, or sensation, that caused hesitation and doubt—doubt not in God but in the serpent. Satan knew her instinct, too. He knew it intimately. As well as God did, in fact. After all, he'd fallen victim to this same nature much earlier in the prequel to this story, and it landed him as a permanent resident of hell.

Satan counted on Adam and Eve to simply follow their nature, too. His slithery path was hard to resist. He enticed them just beyond their reach to a place they knew they shouldn't go. They'd been warned not to cross the boundary. They knew the consequences. God didn't tempt them; their own desire did. The consequence was devastating—much greater than a one-time, mild shock. In fact, the shock is still rippling, thousands of years later. Can you feel it?

> *When Adam sinned, sin entered the world. Adam's sin brought death, so death spread to everyone, for everyone sinned.* (Romans 5:12)

Everyone was impacted—you and me. Yet God is faithful. He continues to praise us, reward us, and affirm us when we obey. He doesn't give up on us; he's cheering us on, applauding us when we resist the desire to go after that thing we want that's just out of our reach.

What thing is just beyond the perimeter of your life? What desire is tempting you to cross the line? Maybe it's the kind of food that tastes so good but is not so good for you. Maybe it's a relationship that you desire but is bad for you. Maybe it's the couch that beckons you to crash on it rather than do the workout that would make you feel better.

Be encouraged today that God has something much better in store for you inside the garden of your life. He knows your nature, and he doesn't tempt you. He wants a life of abundance for you—the kind that leads to eternal life rather than temporal satisfaction. But if you allow yourself to constantly cross the line and run after that temporary desire, you will experience pain. It may be immediate, or it may take a while to take hold of your life.

One of the great problems of pain is that if we experience the same kind enough times, it becomes less painful and more familiar. It's why so many of us can repeatedly walk back into situations that are harmful to us. The circumstance is the same, but our pain threshold, our baseline, has moved. We ignored it, stuffed it down, or didn't attend to it properly, and after a while, we stopped feeling it altogether (usually because we've numbed it with something else).

It's like our conscience. If we "compromise" enough times, we become numb to the same stimulus that caused that little hesitation the first time around. Ignoring the voice of our conscience is like not listening to and honoring the messages that our bodies are sending us all the time—and eventually, the voices just fade away. We become out of touch with our own bodies. It's why we go through so many motions in our days unconsciously, without thinking, without being present and in the moment. Our job is to be present and tune back in. Sometimes we need to remind ourselves to feel the pain again. Pain is inevitable. At some point, life *is* going to hurt a little—or a lot. A storm will come. Knowing that storms are an inevitable part of your life, however, allows you to prepare for them in advance.

Here are three things you can do today to become more resilient for that next temptation storm:

Collect your gear.

If you've ever been camping (still not sure why anyone would *choose* to do such a thing), you know it requires a lot of preparation—loads and loads of it. And rain is always a threat. What gear do you need in case it rains? What "gear" will get you through the tough times in your life? Your Bible? A favorite song that inspires you? How about some great go-to food you've stashed away in your freezer for those crazy days that threaten to send you through the drive-through lane? Or some at-home workout DVDs so you don't miss a workout day when you can't get to the gym? Planning and prepping will help you stay buoyant in rough water.

Gather your storm-riding friends.

When our boys were little and there was a tornado warning, we'd pull them out of bed and huddle with blankets and a radio—and snacks, of course—under our stairwell. As the winds howled and the rain pelted the windows, we'd be crouched tightly together with happy little boys who were excited to be awake after their bedtime. Maybe that's why, to this day, my boys actually like storms. Do you have friends who will cuddle with you during a storm? No matter how hard the wind blows and lightning crashes, we can rest knowing that *"for where two or three gather together as my followers, I am there among them"* (Matthew 18:20).

Start with the end in mind.

There *is* a season of coming out of the storm. There's an ending. I know, keeping perspective is difficult when you're in the throes of a huge, engulfing wave. When your mind-set is established before you're smack-dab in the middle of it, however, you're much more likely to have that comforting reminder of its temporary nature, even if it's just that restless scratch below the surface. Examples? Determine in advance what you will have for dinner. Pack your snacks (and bring them with you) *before* the fight with your boss derails your day and sends you running to the vending machine. Commit to your spouse that you'll be home for dinner so that you won't be overtaken by the temptation to stay at work and unbury yourself from the latest work project. Establishing a mind-set of healthier choices will build your ability to make better choices despite what life inevitably throws at you.

You are empowered and equipped to withstand. In your brokenness, you will find your strength, and you will overcome.

> *Dear friends, don't be surprised at the fiery*
> *trials you are going through, as if something*
> *strange were happening to you. Instead,*
> *be very glad—for these trials make you*
> *partners with Christ in his suffering, so that you*
> *will have the wonderful joy of seeing his glory*
> *when it is revealed to all the world.*
> —1 Peter 4:12-13

LESSON 6:

PAIN IN CHILDBIRTH STINKS

I can tell you as a three-time survivor, childbirth hurts. Sparing you the gory details, each of my sons' births was drastically different. After I had labored for over twenty-six hours with my firstborn, the doctor finally determined that my son had the shoulders of a linebacker and delivered him via C-section. Son number two came at rip-roaring speed, non-C-section-style. I find it ironic that I affectionately call him "Turtle" since he hasn't done anything that fast since.

It took four and a half years before the memories subsided long enough to contemplate another pregnancy and to eventually welcome son number three. Though we considered giving all three boys *A* names (Andrew, Alex, and . . . Kyle), Adam was never in the running. He lost the namesake opportunity with that apple stunt.

I welcomed drugs. Pain was not my friend—epidurals were. I asked for them as quickly as possible and gave thanks for modern medicine! The choices Adam and Eve made back in that garden had consequences we still live with today. Pain in childbirth is one with which women were gifted. Great.

Then the Lord God said to the serpent,

"Because you have done this, you are cursed more than all animals, domestic and wild. You will crawl on your belly, groveling in the dust as long as you live.

And I will cause hostility between you and the woman, and between your offspring and her offspring. He will strike your head, and you will strike his heel."

Then he said to the woman, "I will sharpen the pain of your pregnancy, and in pain you will give birth. And you will desire to control your husband, but he will rule over you."

And to the man he said, "Since you listened to your wife and ate from the tree whose fruit I commanded you not to eat, the ground is cursed because of you. All your life you will struggle to scratch a living from it.

It will grow thorns and thistles for you, though you will eat of its grains. By the sweat of your brow will you have food to eat until you return to the ground from which you were made.
For you were made from dust, and to dust you will return." (Genesis 3:14–19)

Choices are not without consequence. Ever. There is an "if this, then that" connection. It's a ripple effect. Not-so-great choices often bring not-so-great consequences—even pain. Adam and Eve learned this in an instant. For Eve, the consequences were pain in childbirth (physical) and power struggles with Adam (emotional and spiritual). For Adam, the consequences involved hard labor (physical) and animosity with God's creation (emotional and spiritual). Ironically, labor was a shared consequence, though each would experience it differently. I'll let you decide who got the worse end of that one.

Pain is rarely an experience limited solely to the mind, the body, or the spirit. Instead, it's a holistic experience of mind, body, *and* spirit. The three are intimately intertwined and rarely extricable from one another. The mind-body-spirit connection is so strong that emotional pain will frequently manifest itself as physical pain and vice versa. Remember the season of my life when I was struggling with undiagnosed knee pain? A physical answer was never found. My aha moment came when I realized that I was also in a season of unacknowledged emotional turmoil. When I finally addressed *that* pain (detailed in a later chapter), my physical pain subsided considerably. Pain *will* find a way to alleviate itself. It will leak.

We don't like pain. By nature, our bodies fight against it. Biologically, the body is designed to seek the path of least resistance. It's designed to self-preserve and self-protect. When it encounters pain, it seeks the easiest solution. Exercise itself is a difficult, anti–human nature activity. (I know someone out there is shouting, "Amen!") My mom used to say that she'd take up running when she saw a runner smiling. She's still not running.

Exercise forces our bodies to engage in movements that fight gravity, strain our muscles, joints, and organs, and challenge our easy instinct. Movement leads to pain. Yet there are more reasons *to* do it than not, despite having to fight our biological inclinations.

Maybe you've heard the saying "Pain now or pain later." We can feel discomfort from exercising our muscles or from allowing them to stay dormant with inactivity. We can push ourselves to fatigue through a workout or feel the fatigue of lethargy. We pay for the latter choices in the short term through a sore neck, back, and knees, and low mood and energy, or in the long term through cardiovascular disease, diabetes, and other preventable health deteriorations. The prevention of disease, the improvement of cardiac and brain health, and even the stability of our emotions demand physical movement. We are healthier, inside and out, when we move. Pain is inevitable. You choose your pain.

There's a caveat, however, to connecting exercise with pain. Exercise should never be a form of self-punishment. For example, we should not inflict pain on ourselves because we ate the "wrong" thing or ate "too much." We shouldn't beat ourselves up with extreme workouts, pushing ourselves to the brink of exhaustion so that we feel better about our bodies or about a choice we made with our nutrition. It's easy to do. We come by this inclination naturally. Once again, we see the pattern begin in the Garden of Eden. Adam and Eve ate a forbidden food, something "bad," and were punished for their choice. We have inadvertently brought the bad-choice-equals-punishment equation into our modern-day lives. But there's a foundational problem with this. We are not God.

Because of the actions of Adam and Eve, God responded with the punishment he had promised. A good, faithful, and just God could do nothing less. The fruit just happened to be the object of their disobedience, the unfortunate scapegoat. God's problem wasn't with the fruit; it was with Adam's and Eve's hearts.

We have fallen into the trap, however, of taking it upon ourselves to view *food* as good or bad and to force upon ourselves the "consequence" of making a bad choice. This punishment can take the form of self-restriction, deprivation or withholding of food (can you say *dieting*?), or forcing ourselves to work out harder or longer. See if you can relate to these statements:

"I ate (blank), so I'm going to do an extra fifteen minutes on the elliptical machine."

"I am going to drink (blank) at the party tonight, so I'd better get to the gym today."

"I can't believe I ate (blank). I'm going to get up thirty minutes earlier tomorrow to go for an extra-long run."

"I ate (blank). I have no self-control and will never lose weight."

We do it ourselves. We play God. Unfortunately, some personal trainers can fall into this trap, too. Punishment can be easily disguised as "motivation." I witnessed it firsthand sometimes while working alongside other trainers in a health club. You, too, have seen it if you ever watched *The Biggest Loser*. Jillian Michaels' endless tirades in the name of "helping" are legendary.

As a small group training instructor, I was an accomplice as well. The workout program assigned for us to lead at the health club the day after Thanksgiving was designed around what and how much was eaten during the previous day of feasting. Though intended as a lighthearted, fun workout, each food was assigned a "punishment" of push-ups, sit-ups, burpees, and more. Participants paid a price for eating "unhealthy" traditional Thanksgiving foods. Instead of continuing to give thanks, group members were more than likely cursing us, and themselves, by the end of class. I will reiterate here that this workout was *not* designed to be mean-spirited, but it did reinforce our complicated relationship with food and exercise.

Self-punishment is neither motivational nor effective. When we feel the need to force exercise on ourselves as retribution for the necessary act of eating, something's gotten off-kilter. When God designed our bodies to move in ways that can keep them healthy and fit, it was never his intent to inflict punishment on us. We may not always love to exercise, but it should never be a self-inflicted indictment of a "bad" choice we made or of the way we feel about ourselves. Is exercise painful sometimes? Yes. Is it hard sometimes? Yes. But we are called to do hard things sometimes.

> *No discipline is enjoyable while it's happening—it's painful! But afterward there will be a peaceful harvest of right living for those who are trained in this way.* (Hebrews 12:11)

In our shortsightedness, we often choose easy, not hard. We are tempted, daily, to sit still. To overcome this innate inclination, we can put physics to work for us. I'm not a science geek, but I have firsthand experience of Newton's first law of motion. This principle simply states the following:

> Every object in a state of uniform motion tends to remain in that state of motion unless an external force is applied to it. This is also known as the law of inertia.

Why does this matter? To borrow Nike's slogan, "Just Do It." In other words, if you simply start moving, you are more likely to continue moving than you are to stop. If you start with one push-up, you're more likely to do two. If you start with a five-minute workout, you're more likely to do fifteen. It's harder to stop than it is to continue. Allow science to work for you! Anything is better than nothing. It's so easy to set ourselves up for failure in this area of our lives. We demand too much. We try to go from no exercise, literally zero, to a six- or seven-day workout regimen each week. If—and that's a big *if*—we make it to the end of week one, how likely is it that we'll continue for the entire ninety days? Or a lifetime?

Monday is "National Do-Over Day." Every Monday, we promise ourselves that *this* week, *this* time, it will be different. We buy new shoes or a new outfit or a new DVD hoping *that* will be the key. We join a gym only to find ourselves hitting the Snooze button in the morning or driving past the health club parking lot after a busy day.

What if you did something different? What if you started small? What if instead of trying to fit in a thirty-minute (or longer) daily workout, you simply did five push-ups or went for a five-minute walk? What if you committed to taking one hundred more steps per day or taking the stairs instead of the elevator whenever you could? What if you parked farther from the store entrance (okay, maybe not in Minnesota in January) or walked your child to school? These little changes in our daily lives have physical, emotional, and even spiritual benefits.

First, we get our bodies moving. Period. Any added movement is an improvement. Even adding one small activity to a regular exercise routine can yield big results.

Second, we feel better. Our endorphins get moving, yes, but we also feel like we've done something that's good for us. We begin to establish a pattern of successful movement. When we start practicing an established activity on a regular basis and actually *do it*, we succeed at a small goal instead of failing at a big one. (Remember those unused DVDs on your shelf?)

Finally, we can use the time to connect with God. A five-minute walk can be a conversation with him. The time you're walking up the steps at work can be a time to thank him for the body he's given you. (Or maybe a time to ask for his help to make it to the tenth floor!) Each push-up or lap in the pool could be a reminder to pray for someone, by name, in your life. Body, mind, and spirit benefit from the movement we build into our lives. When one is healthy, the others are more likely to benefit as well.

Setting up your environment for success is crucial for making these changes easier. If you have to step over dumbbells every time you want to sit on the couch, you're more likely to choose to hit Play on that workout DVD than watch the latest episode of your favorite show. Or better yet, how about if you use those dumbbells *while* you're watching television. For a period of time, I *only* watched a recorded show or movie when I was on the treadmill. I'd hit Pause on the remote after thirty minutes or so, which motivated me to get back on the treadmill to catch the rest of the episode or film later.

Similarly, if your goal is to eat more fruits and vegetables, keeping them readily accessible on the counter will make it more likely you'll grab those than hunt through your pantry for the nonperishables that are not so great for you at 9:00 p.m. Restocking your refrigerator regularly with plenty of healthy options is also a helpful environmental tweak to establish a healthier eating pattern.

Just as important is staying away from environments that are not going to help you reach your goal. If you are constantly faced with temptation, you are lowering your odds of making any kind of significant life change. God didn't pull any punches with Adam and Eve. He evicted them from their home.

> So the Lord God banished them from the Garden of Eden, and he sent Adam out to cultivate the ground from which he had been made. After sending them out, the Lord God stationed mighty cherubim to the east of the Garden of Eden. And he placed a flaming sword that flashed back and forth to guard the way to the tree of life. (Genesis 3:23–24)

God put up the invisible fence of all invisible fences. It was crystal clear. Off limits for good. As strange as it seems, he showed amazing grace by doing so. He could have ended Adam's and Eve's lives on the spot. Instead, he chose life for them, but it would be the harder kind of life. They no longer had easy nourishment at their fingertips, harmonious relationships with the Garden's creatures, or beautiful scenery in which to bask. And, most significantly, it was life apart from the presence of God—the most devastating consequence of all.

What's separating you from God? What do you need to banish from your life? Maybe it's a location, like a bar or a friend's house where you know alcohol will flow freely. Maybe it's a food that triggers a landslide of binging. Maybe it's a person—a "basement dweller" friend or family member whose presence carries with it all kinds of emotional baggage that takes you to negative or dark places.

Set the flaming swords ablaze! Call on God's help to do so because he's got angels to help guard the entrance to that place of temptation and desire. And get moving. The better the environment that you create for yourself and the better the path that you pave toward your ultimate health goal, the more successful you'll be, today and tomorrow.

Here are three ways you can learn to love (or at least tolerate) exercise and avoid "bad pain":

Make it chunky.
An upcoming wedding, reunion, or trip are great motivators to get in shape. They provide the little boost we need to get started, but be ever so careful not to stop when that occasion has come and gone. Once the target date has passed, find a *new* something to work toward. Maybe it's a new outfit you'd like to buy, or a weekend away with a friend or spouse,

or a Kelly Clarkson concert. (Or is that just *me*?) Make the motivators specific and in the near future (thirty to sixty days). These short-term, reachable milestones will help keep you moving in a healthier direction.

Play it forward.
Tune in to the way you feel now . . . then envision your preferred future. How will you *feel* when you reach that new weight? How will your relationship with yourself change? How will a healthier you impact your family? If you fast-forward your life and like what you see, don't change a thing. But if what you see scares or concerns you, commit to changing that future. Allow the picture of your preferred future to motivate you to make changes. Your future starts with the choices you make today.

Think outside the box.
For some, a traditional exercise program will never be the right fit. Pushing Play on a DVD player or going to the gym will always feel like torture. So be creative. Garden, clean your house with vigor, ride your bike, take dance lessons. Expand your definition of exercise, and move. If you don't love it, you won't do it. Period. If you hate running, you won't stick with it. If you hate to dance, then Zumba won't grab you. But make sure you experiment. Try new things—more than once. Give it at least three times to make a true assessment. You just may discover your inner marathoner or future *Dancing with the Stars* contestant. If you don't, move on—seriously, *move on*. Your soul mate workout is waiting for you.

Getting, or staying, in shape is *not* easy. It may be one of the hardest things you'll ever do. Would it be easier to sleep in, avoid the DVDs or gym, and skip the workout? No doubt. But I know that when I do that, I'm more sore than when I don't exercise. I'm still in pain—the hip-popping, back-cracking, snaps-and-pops kind that comes as the days and years go by. Pain is inevitable. Choose the "good" kind.

> *She is clothed with strength and dignity,*
> *and she laughs without fear of the future.*
> *When she speaks, her words are wise,*
> *and she gives instructions with kindness.*
> *She carefully watches everything in her*
> *household and suffers nothing from laziness.*
> —Proverbs 31:25-27

LESSON 7:

FOOD IS NOT A MORAL ISSUE

We like labels. We prefer black and white, right and wrong, good or bad. Categorizing gives us a sense of order and control when we're met daily with an abundance of choices, options, and decisions. Food is no different. We're told to eat this, not that. We talk about good and bad foods, healthy and unhealthy choices, and we make our decisions using these polarizing terms. But food matters can be gray.

Never is this more apparent than when I talk with someone during our first nutrition coaching session. Anxiety over food is generally at its peak during this initial conversation. People are so confused about the conflicting information they hear about what to eat, what to avoid, and everything in between. Sometimes they're frustrated because they feel like they're doing all the "right" things yet are not seeing results on the holy grail of health: the scale.

I do my best to walk new clients through a very intentional discovery process to get to know them better. Understanding their past and present relationship with food helps me gather information about their future desires and goals. Most people are relatively willing, accommodating, and transparent when I ask questions, but some simply don't want to answer them. They want to ask them.

Sometimes coaching sessions feel like a pinball game, with my only goal being to prevent the ball from dropping through the perilous hole. With rapid-fire questioning, I'm drilled about what foods are "good" and "bad." I'm bounced from one danger food to another with no specific direction or intentional path. I don't like this game.

In one such standout session, no matter how hard I tried, I simply could not get the conversation back on track. After asking "Sandy" a question, I'd get a brief reply followed by, "What I really want to know is . . ." I spent almost the entire session answering, "It depends," and trying to explain the answer. After forty minutes of fighting back complete exasperation (and exhaustion), I said, "I'll try to make this very simple. If it grows in the ground or on a tree, eat it. Eat it in abundance."

Two breaths later, she asked, "So, what about Lean Cuisine?" For real. Without skipping a beat, she continued to plunge ahead, peppering me with non-plant- and non-tree-based food questions before I finally escorted her out of my office, fifteen minutes after our allotted time. Much to my chagrin, I ran into her on my way out of the building. She cornered me again, saying, "We forgot to talk about Diet Coke. That's bad, isn't it?" I wanted to scream, "Does Diet Coke grow on a tree?" I didn't. I'm not always that patient.

Sandy didn't like gray. In the Garden, however, the choice Adam and Eve had before them *was* black and white, right or wrong, good or bad. There were consequences for the choice they made that had a life-altering impact.

> *The Lord God placed the man in the Garden of Eden to tend and watch over it. But the Lord God warned him, "You may freely eat the fruit of every tree in the garden—except the tree of the knowledge of good and evil. If you eat its fruit, you are sure to die."* (Genesis 2:15–17)

The off-limit, do-not-touch object of desire in the Garden just happened to be a piece of fruit. It could have been anything. It could have been a banana, pineapple, or coconut. It could have been a hamburger, a pizza, or chicken wings. A cake, a cookie, or peanut butter cups (just me?) could have hung from that tree, or a case of beer, bottle of wine, or Diet Coke. Pick your apple. We all have at least one thing that entices us and calls us. It's the thing that tempts us to compromise. Despite the warning, we reach, grab, and eat.

We ignore the warning chirps. We look past the elevated blood pressure, blood sugar, or cholesterol numbers. We eschew the escalating number on the scale, the increasing belt size, or the zipper that no longer zips. Instead, we listen to the subtle *hissssss* saying, "Is it *really* that bad? Can you *really* not have anything fun to eat? Just this once . . ." And we bite.

God gave us choice. He created us with the will to choose. A loving God couldn't do it any other way. Would mandating us to love him be a loving thing to do? Is using force a good way to show love? Without choice, there is no love. He knows that sometimes we'll make a decision that is less than ideal for us. We'll choose things that will harm us, hurt us, and cause us pain. We'll make decisions that take us further away from optimal health and closer to disease. Does this hurt him? Yes. But it hurts us more. Adam and Eve's decision hurt them, but it wasn't the result of a bad apple; the fruit simply revealed the condition of their hearts.

It's interesting that despite the apple's role in our depraved condition today, we've never blamed the fruit itself. It's never had a "bad" label—quite the contrary, really. We consider apples to be one of the healthiest of all food choices, even espousing its virtues by encouraging daily consumption with the well-known phrase "An apple a day keeps the doctor away." From a purely nutritional perspective, it's a nutrient-dense, power-packed food that supports our health. But rather than putting foods into categories like "good" and "bad," let's put them on a continuum. On the better end of the continuum are foods that lead us closer to health, and on the other end are ones that take us further from it. For optimal health, we can borrow food researcher and journalist Michael Pollan's advice:

Eat food. Not too much. Mostly plants.

It can be that simple, but simple isn't always easy. Pollan's advice is not an all-or-nothing philosophy. It's a suggestion to eat as much real food as possible (the stuff that grows in nature) and to eat it in moderation. Just enough to reach satiety. Even with that advice, we still must be careful not to make this a black-and-white, plants-or-nothing world. We need to stop polarizing and moralizing food.

With Pollan's seven simple words, we have a guideline, a continuum, for choosing the foods that lead us toward health instead of away from it. The closer a food is to its original, natural state, the closer it is to the better end of the spectrum of food choices. The further away it is from its natural state, the less beneficial it is for our bodies. The food industry is guilty of taking God's crops and turning them into food-like substances that are virtually unrecognizable from real food. Sometimes I feel like processed food is our vain attempt to say, "You know what, God? I've got this. I'll make something better than you did." A more responsible choice would be concentrating our efforts on choosing God's original foods as often as possible.

Let me fill in the gaps just a little bit more. I've developed this acronym for making healthy choices less complicated:

SIMPLE.

Slow down. In our drive-through world, it's easy to eat on the run. Even healthy food can cause indigestion if eaten too quickly. Sit for twenty minutes (or more) at a meal, try chewing your food twenty times before swallowing (it's hard!), or wake twenty minutes earlier to enjoy breakfast instead of rushing out the door. This step alone can make a monumental difference in your relationship with food and the choices you make.

Investigate. If it has a label, can you pronounce the ingredients? Do you know what they are? If you can't, put it back on the shelf. Better yet, avoid the foods with labels. An apple is an apple. A pear is a pear. Real food doesn't need labels, but when the occasion calls for a can, a box, or a bag, know what's in it.

Measure. Use your hand as your portion guide. A clenched fist is a cup of fruits, veggies, or carbs. An open palm is a protein serving. Your thumb is a serving of healthy fat. (Yes, including peanut butter!) You don't need calorie counting, points, or scales to eat what your body needs. Your body is your guide.

Plants. Eat them—lots of them. Half your plate should be filled with these nutritional powerhouses in every meal of the day (yes, including breakfast!). Go heavier on the veggies and lighter on the fruits if your goal is weight loss. But, if it grows in the ground or on a tree, it's ideal for meeting the bulk of your body's nutritional needs. Think Garden of Eden. If it grew there or roamed there, God made it just for you. Just be careful for that one apple . . .

Lean proteins. Grass-fed beef, chicken, fish (especially salmon), and pork all provide a variety of awesome protein sources for your body. Front-loading with proteins is a good way to offset our love affair with carb-filled breakfast options like pancakes, bagels, cereal, or toast. Eggs, Greek yogurt, and even bacon will fire you up and keep you full longer. If you're a woman and want to give your metabolism a kick in the pants, protein is your best friend, along with healthy fats. Incorporate them into every meal and snack, every day.

Eat intuitively. Listen to your body signaling when it's time to eat. Don't put meals and snacks off when you start feeling those hunger pangs. For many of us, that means eating every three to four hours throughout the day. Your blood sugar levels (and energy) remain steady, cravings stay at bay, and you'll be less likely to overeat in the evening when your body is demanding food!

It really can be **SIMPLE**. Yes, there are nuances to food. There are fruits that have less sugar, proteins that are leaner than others, carbs that are more nutrient dense, and so on, and there are times when this matters, but most of the time it doesn't. If you're looking for a solid foundation without overcomplicating and overwhelming yourself with a whole lot of "eat this, not that," think SIMPLE.

I totally understand when clients ask questions. I'm more than happy to provide clarity in a nutritional world that has been made very, very confusing. It's my job as someone who has studied nutrition and whose role is to coach others. I'd just rather not be used as a nutritional encyclopedia. Or Siri.

Ultimately, here's my advice: If you want to eat something, eat it. If you don't, don't. The choice is yours. The Bible doesn't give us a lot of specific information about what we should or shouldn't eat; we just know that our health will be better if we stay away from certain things. Just pay attention to how you feel when you eat the foods you do. Learn to listen to your body by eating slowly and intentionally. Your body will guide you. Some questions to ask yourself are:

Do I feel content and satisfied? Or do I feel stuffed or deprived?

Do I feel energized? Or do I feel sluggish and ready for a nap?

Do I feel focused? Or do I feel foggy?

This awareness of how you feel will help you intuitively recognize how food impacts not only your physical body but your emotional state as well.

Detach yourself from some of the judgments you've cast on foods in the past. Healthy eating shouldn't feel like punishment. You're not relegated to a life of celery and carrot sticks! You can enjoy things like dessert and coffee and alcohol. Just do it consciously. Do it by choice instead of compulsion or craving. Food should not be a source of shame. I'd be independently wealthy if I had a penny for every time someone said they "cheated" or ate a "bad" food. We've been so conditioned to be hard on ourselves when we don't make a "good" choice all the time. Who wants to live that way?

We can *all* be normal eaters. There are no hard and fast rules for what "normal" eating looks like. That's the wonderful and amazing thing about choices. We get to customize what works for us. By paying attention to our emotional and physiological response to food, we will be able to eat without the feelings of guilt that often accompany it.

Karen Koenig is a licensed psychotherapist, motivational speaker, and international author who has specialized in the field of compulsive, emotional, and restrictive eating for more than thirty years. She identifies four simple rules that "normal" eaters adhere to:[8]

1. Eating when they're hungry or have a craving.

2. Choosing foods that will intuitively satisfy them.

3. Eating with awareness and enjoyment.

4. Stopping eating when they're full or satisfied.

"Normal" is in quotes for a reason. There is no one definition of a normal eating pattern. Some people *can* eat only two or three times a day while others eat five or six, and both can have a healthy relationship with food. Notice that the rules aren't about a specific pattern, timing, or quantity. Body awareness undergirds all the principles.

Let's dive into this a little more specifically, starting with rule one. If you're a "normal" eater, you will understand and listen to your body's cues. You will notice when you are hungry versus thirsty or hungry versus anxious, for example. You may or may not eat when you feel a craving. If you do indulge the craving, it will be in moderate amounts, like enjoying a small piece of chocolate (key word: *small*!). Or you may choose to recognize it and move on. You feel in control of your choice.

Rule two is about knowing what your body truly needs in each moment. If you're about to work out, for example, you eat to fuel that workout for your best performance, or if you are exceptionally hungry, you will eat something hearty to satisfy that hunger. Food is more than fuel, but it functions as such when we need it.

Rule three allows you to truly experience food. Noticing the texture, taste, and fragrance of the foods you eat allows you to more intuitively make choices about foods you thoroughly enjoy and, more importantly, that your *body* enjoys. Your body will signal which ones it likes (good energy, mood, performance) and which ones it doesn't (low energy, mood, performance).

Rule four is trickier. Knowing when you're content versus full takes practice and a willingness to work against our inclination to eat quickly. It takes time to get to know what 80 percent full feels like, but this is the optimal level of satiety for your body. With patience and focused attention, however, you will begin to know when you feel "just right" and quit eating.

So, now the important question: How normal are you? If you're anything like me, you're semi-normal. You probably have at least one attribute of a normal eater, but you may struggle with the rest. Or maybe you are normal in most respects and only struggle with one. Remember, the goal is not perfect eating. Rather, it's practicing new food habits, or behaviors, so that you can live a healthier life. We redefine our relationships with food through the choices we make every single day, resulting in neither obsession nor apathy with what we consume.

Isabel Foxen Duke, an emotional-eating health coach, puts it this way:

> "Normies" don't have a line to cross. If they eat a big dinner, they eat a big dinner. No big deal. If they have a cupcake in the middle of the day for no reason, they eat a cupcake and move on with their lives. If they eat an entire bag of chips in a sitting, they eat the bag and then think "ugh I need water," and get over it. What they eat has NO bearing on their self-esteem. It means nothing.[9]

Some days, we will be a "normie." We will feel successful. Other days, we will feel like we didn't do *anything* right. But if you're living and breathing at the end of the day, you didn't do everything wrong either. And tomorrow's a new day.

What if instead of perfection, we aimed for "good enough"? Initially, this concept may create a bit of tension for you, like it did for me. I've always had a desire for excellence in everything I do. It's one of my core values.

But then I realized these two concepts, *good enough* and *excellence*, can play nicely together. *Good enough* doesn't mean compromising quality. It means doing your best, in the moment, every day. It means committing to change but doing what you can—in real life. And real life doesn't always allow us to eat perfectly, exercise perfectly, or relate perfectly. Does this mean we're less excellent? I'd argue no. In fact, by letting go of our pursuit of perfection, we allow for *greater excellence and better balance* in more areas of our lives.

Consider this: If we spend all our time pursuing the perfect body, do we compromise time with people we love? If we demand perfect nutrition of ourselves at all times and in all situations, do we miss out on the pleasure of an amazing dessert or a gourmet meal prepared by someone whose personal excellence and glorification of God comes through his or her gift of cooking?

In short, the pursuit of perfection leads to failure every time. Sure, we may see short-term gains or successes. We may have a perfect eating day or a perfect workout. We may have a perfect conversation in a difficult situation or a perfect date. But these unyielding expectations lead us to disappointment and discouragement in the long term. *Good enough*, on the other hand, is sustainable for life, for good, for real. And it releases all the pressure and stress of failing.

Here are three ways to start eating, and living, good enough right now:

Control only what you can control.
In each of our lives, we have three circles of control; the things we have *total* control over, the things we have *some* control over, and the things we have *no* control over. So much stress is a result of trying to control too many things in the *some*

and *no* areas of our lives. As a result, we deflect our power of choice (remember that finger-wagging?). Focus instead on what you have *total* control over. You may not be able to control what is offered to you on a buffet, for example, but you do have total control over what you choose from that buffet. You can't control what restaurant is chosen when you're part of a work team or social group, but you do have total control over what selection you make from that menu (and can "pass" on shared appetizers or desserts you'd prefer not to eat). You can make a "good enough" choice when you aren't in total control of your situation.

Set realistic expectations.

I hate to break it to you, but it takes longer than twenty-one days to create a new habit. Hard ones, like nutrition and exercise, can take a year . . . or more. The good news is that habit-building is progressive. Just because you can't conquer your weight-loss goals in a day doesn't mean you can't make positive changes today. Remember those short-term goals we talked about earlier in this book? Use those to keep motivated, but commit for the long term. Practice the skills that will lead you to your goal so that even if you don't get to your ideal destination, you will have built healthier habits along the way.

Rinse and repeat.

Prepare to practice what you want to achieve. Do it over and over again. There's a reason I talk about this principle repeatedly. We need repetition to make something stick. The more we hear something or the more we repeat a behavior, habit, or method that we want to become second nature, the more second nature it will become. The more it will sink in. The most successful transformations I've seen in clients happen when they commit to doing some things differently day in and day out. And they're kind to themselves when they have a "bad" day. We become what we repeatedly do, so hit the Replay button!

Good enough really is the best way to see lasting lifestyle change through small, daily, doable action steps. *Good enough* is good enough. In fact, it's perfect.

That is why I tell you not to worry about
everyday life—whether you have enough food
and drink, or enough clothes to wear.
Isn't life more than food,
and your body more than clothing?
—Matthew 6:25

LESSON 8:

WE WANT WHAT WE CAN'T HAVE

I hate GameStop. I have done more battles because of that store than I have in any other retail establishment on the planet. Even Target, with all its many temptations for young and old, pales in comparison to the wars that have resulted from video games.

Like a lot of kids his age, Alex was drawn to doing what his friends were doing. It started innocently enough with Pokémon cards in elementary school (the nontechnical precursor to *Pokémon Go*) and escalated to M-rated (Mature) video games in middle school. Unfortunately, I couldn't rely on the "well, *we* make different choices because of our faith" speech because a lot of his Christian friends were being allowed to play these mature games. This became a huge point of contention in our never-ending dialogue about gaming.

Being somewhat reasonable (at least in our minds), we gave Alex a chance to present his case when we disagreed. He shared his best, logical argument for why he should be allowed to do something that we didn't feel he should. During his Pokémon cards lawyering, he eventually won. He got the reluctant go-ahead from me. (And he still doesn't let me forget it!)

Mature video games were another story. No matter how many arguments he made, we wouldn't budge. Sometimes I'd agree to take him to GameStop so he could purchase a compromised-upon T-rated (Teen) game. But inevitably, once in the store, the pleading would begin. And I'd be back in the yogurt aisle, this time with child number two. The colicky one. This was his time to explode.

"Alex, do you want this video game or this one?" He always pointed to the one on the shelf. I don't know why I thought it would work *this* time, with *this* child. Even if Alex's intent wasn't to draw us into a potential *yes* in that store, once inside, he was tempted beyond what his still growing heart and mind could stand. The games beckoned when they were within his grasp. Some of our biggest head-to-head, parent-child battles occurred on the heels of those store visits and sometimes in the store. Yogurt aisle times ten. Same desire, different child.

Alex wanted what he couldn't have. *Call of Duty* was his apple.

Eve wanted what was in front of her, too. She wanted the thing she couldn't have. Do you think she bargained with God? Do you think she created a PowerPoint or Excel spreadsheet with data, statistics, and arguments? Did she neatly write her words in the dirt, explaining why God had it all wrong? Did she negotiate, plead, yell, or scream? Did she hover ever so near that M-rated fruit, hoping maybe God would change his mind? Did she hope being in proximity to the fruit would force God's hand (because he wouldn't want to make a scene) and cause him to change his mind? I wonder.

When Alex was at sleepovers, out of our sight, he'd play those forbidden games. He'd come home and confess that he'd played them, though these confessions weren't overt or voluntary. We'd seek him out and ask, even when we already knew the answer. We'd find him in his room, wearing his holey jacket. When confronted, most often he'd wag his finger.

"All the other kids were playing."

"I tried not to play, but they were making fun of me for not playing."

"So-and-so's mom lets him play. And they're a Christian family." (Ouch!)

We could see through the fig leaves, and he didn't like it. We empathized with him, knowing what it was like to want to fit in and share experiences with friends. He knew that when he got older, he would get to play the games he desired. We didn't even mandate that he wait until he was seventeen, the recommended age for such games. But Alex didn't want to wait. He wanted to play *now*. Much to Alex's chagrin, Kyle has won similar gaming wars at a much younger age thanks to battle-weary parents. We understood then, and now, that waiting feels like an eternity when something enticing is dangling in front of you.

One of the longest-running studies in human psychology is simply called the Marshmallow Experiment. If you haven't seen the videos from this study, look them up on YouTube and be prepared to laugh . . . and learn.

In short, a series of experiments were done over several years in the 1960s and 1970s with preschool children at Stanford University's Bing Nursery School. Children ages four to six were put in a room with a marshmallow or other treat of their choice, such as mini-pretzels, mints, or cookies. They were given simple instructions. Eat the treat immediately or wait for up to twenty minutes and get a second treat. Each child was then left alone in the room alongside a bell they could ring at any time to call the researcher back to the room so they could eat the one treat and forgo the bonus. All of this was recorded through a two-way mirror.

In all the combined studies, only about one-third of the participants delayed gratification and were rewarded with the second treat.[10] The study raised many questions about willpower and other inborn tendencies, but one similarity was noted. Many of those who "failed" by eating the marshmallow before the researcher returned put themselves smack-dab in front of temptation. They smelled the marshmallow. They stared at it. Touched it. Flipped it. Even licked it. Eventually, they ate it.

A marshmallow or mint may not be *your* idea of temptation, but I bet you have a stand-in. Chocolate chip cookies, pizza, McDonald's french fries, peanut butter . . . oh, wait. That's my one, two, three, four . . . Whatever it is, something beckons to us. Something whispers from a kitchen plate, from behind a grocery counter, or from a restaurant menu. It promises instant gratification. Sugary sweet sensations. Salty satisfaction. Delightfully delicious dough.

Like children, we may resist . . . for a while. Only a small handful of the kids in the Stanford study dove right in and indulged in the fluffy goodness. Most waited for a while. But during the waiting period, they used every ounce of their willpower. Researchers noted that the children would "cover their eyes with their hands or turn around so that they couldn't see the tray, [while] others started kicking the desk, or tugging on their pigtails, or stroking the marshmallow as if it were a tiny stuffed animal."[11]

What are you stroking? I can usually resist freshly baked chocolate chip cookies . . . at first. But the less distance I place between them and me, the greater the desire becomes and the more my willpower weakens. Though I may start in a different room of the house, the closer I get to the kitchen, the harder it is to say no. Eventually, even if my intent was simply to grab a glass of water, my hand will reach for that delightful cookie, and I will devour it.

Popcorn? Same story. The smell alone is intoxicating. And movie theater popcorn? Fuggedaboutit!

In the marshmallow studies, the children who resisted temptation chose a different path from that of the others. After ogling it for a while, they eventually used a strikingly similar strategy. They reframed the situation. They imagined something different to remove the strength of the emotional temptation. Some pictured the marshmallow as a cloud while others put a "picture frame" around it to make it less real. [12] Others simply closed their eyes, putting it out of sight. They didn't smell it or lick it. They resisted what they wanted now by picturing something much better ahead. They trusted the promise of the guy in charge. The researcher made a promise. A better something would come from waiting, by being patient, by delaying gratification. Was it tempting? Yes. Was it hard? Yes. Was it doable? Some thought so.

God promised a better future, too.

> *Then God blessed them and said, "Be fruitful and multiply. Fill the earth and govern it. Reign over the fish in the sea, the birds in the sky, and all the animals that scurry along the ground."*

> *Then God said, "Look! I have given every seed-bearing plant throughout the earth and all the fruit trees for your food. And I have given every green plant as food for all the wild animals, the birds in the sky, and the small animals that scurry the ground—everything that has life."*

> *And that is what happened. Then God looked over all he had made, and he saw that it was very good!* (Genesis 1:28-31)

God's creation of Adam and Eve was the *only* thing in all his handiwork that was deemed "very good." It earned the exclamation point! He had in mind an ideal picture of perfect relational harmony between humans and Himself, humans and his Creation, and between man and woman. He knew the potential for an idyllic life. Adam and Eve had every opportunity to flourish . . . if only they could resist the marshmallow. If they had pictured a better future, they could have enjoyed the payoff for all eternity. God wanted to reward their desire, their obedience, and their trust. He wanted to praise them for their patience and faith. Unfortunately, only *God* pictured their future, their greater reward. Adam and Eve did not. They were distracted. They couldn't see beyond the sight, smell, and enticement of that one tree, that one fruit.

Like Alex standing in GameStop, they could have chosen *Super Mario Kart*, *Backyard Baseball*, or *LEGO Star Wars*. They could have picked from dozens, maybe hundreds, of options.

Their garden abundance may have even included cacao. Yes, chocolate! They could have savored delicious chocolatey goodness. But they just couldn't stop staring at or smelling the fruit of that centrally located tree. They were completely fixated. They wanted to play *Call of Duty* while eating marshmallows—right now.

Interesting insights came from the Stanford marshmallow experiments and other similar tests that followed. After forty years of follow-up studies, the researchers learned that the children who delayed gratification, the ones who resisted the marshmallow or cookies, had higher SAT scores, lower levels of substance abuse, lower likelihood of obesity, better responses to stress, better social skills (as reported by their parents), and generally better scores in a range of other life measures.

Imagine what life would have been like for Adam and Eve if they had just closed their eyes and pictured their promised future. This desire for instant gratification and wanting what we can't have has carried over into the lives of all of Adam and Eve's descendants. The Bible catalogs numerous examples:

> *Esau sold his birthright for a single meal.* (Genesis 25:33)

> *David desired Bathsheba. So he slept with her to fulfill his desire, though she was another man's wife.* (2 Samuel 11:2-4)

> *Abraham was impatient with Sarah's inability to have children, so he slept with Hagar to fulfill what he believed was God's promise.* (Genesis 16:1-3)

> *The rich man's son wanted his inheritance immediately. He squandered it and returned to his father broke and broken.* (Luke 15:13)

We're left with the fallout. Our nature will always lead us into temptation, desire, and wanting what we can't have. But we're also encouraged that trusting in and remaining faithful to the promises of God, drawing on his strength and power, can provide us with greater courage to make hard decisions.

Here are three things you can do today to resist the marshmallow:

Run like Forrest Gump.
Sometime in my childhood, my mom, dad, sister, and I

started using a single word to escape a bad situation: *flee!* I don't even remember how it started, but with that single word we'd encourage one another and others (including characters on television or in movies that we'd talk to through the screen) to get the heck out of there. My husband and I still use that phrase to this day when we see or hear of people putting themselves in precarious situations. Sometimes you must spin on your heels and run as fast as you can. Get out of the kitchen, avoid the road that takes you by the fast-food joints, take a different route at work if you're prone to giving in to the vending machine. If alcohol is your vice, don't even opt in for a single drink if one will lead to two, three, or more.

Use the buddy system.
Accountability is underrated. Good partners make us better people. Great spouses challenge us to be just a little bit better every day. Bad partners bring out the worst in us. Ever notice how easy it is to gossip when others are doing it? Similarly, having a "someone else" who has similar goals and abilities can help keep us on track with our food choices and our exercise habits. Eve was tempted when she was alone. What if Adam had been by her side while the snake was weaving his sordid web of deception? What would have happened if he had shouted, "Flee!"?

Play it forward . . . and go BIG.
What's the best-case scenario? What's the worst? Just like those Choose Your Own Adventure books, there are good and bad endings. When deciding about a choice you're making today, go big. Be extreme. Is this going to be the best experience *ever*? Or is this one little teeny-tiny choice going to wreak havoc for the rest of your life and others' lives? Is this going to hurt your life or help your life? That

simple visualization exercise will help you see more clearly when you're living in the temporal here and now.

Sometimes we get so caught up in "it's just a little thing" that we lose perspective on the big thing. One bite. One drink. One glance. But remember. One choice matters. A lot.

*By his divine power, God has given us
everything we need for living a godly life. We
have received all of this by coming to know
him, the one who called us to himself by means
of his marvelous glory and excellence.*
—2 Peter 1:3

LESSON 9:

WE'RE LOOKING AT THE WRONG REFLECTION

My husband eats out a lot. His job requires him to socialize with colleagues on a semi-regular basis. Kevin has become familiar with the ins and outs of a wide variety of restaurants—the food, the prices, the service, and yes, even the bathrooms.

On a visit to a restaurant in downtown Minneapolis several years ago, he experienced a most unique, and shocking, bathroom design. What should have been a predictable experience was anything but for a new patron like himself. He entered the appropriate door marked for men and took care of business. When he approached the sink, however, he looked up and was startled to see a woman returning his panicked stare! Unbeknownst to him, the sink area was shared between the men's and women's rooms. After his initial disorientation, he realized that he was, in fact, in the right space and was the victim of a very strange (yet humorous) design choice. The reflection he was expecting with a quick "How's my hair?" and "Do I have anything in my teeth?" check was not the one he saw.

Sometimes, we are upended by something as simple as a reflection. We get accustomed to normal patterns and habits. Then one day, we glance up and are jolted by the unexpected—a reflection that's not what we expected to see, a different truth before us. After the initial shock, it's as though the steam-covered mirror suddenly clears and we see what's been there all along—an intended design, but one we almost missed in the fog of routine. We realize we've spent far too much time living in the mist.

> *How do you know what your life will be like tomorrow? Your life is like the morning fog—it's here a little while, then it's gone.* (James 4:14)

Our physical bodies are temporary. I know this. Yet, my body and the time I commit to keeping it healthy consume much more of me than I'd like to admit. Instead of remembering who I'm made to be and what I'm uniquely made to do on earth, I get distracted by my present "imperfections." Though I want to live fully present and engaged in day-to-day life, I veer off course when I become body-focused. I fixate on the temporal. Whether it's the number on the scale, an unflattering picture, or a passing glance in the mirror (at my legs, of course), these distractions can ruin my mood for an entire day—or longer. I get caught up in my appearance.

As a health and wellness coach, it's hard to escape this body focus. I'm constantly encouraged to "be a product of the product." I'm pressured to be a good example of fitness and weight management so that others will be inspired to buy what I'm selling. Without offering proof that what I'm "peddling" works, I'm warned I might not be very successful. And, if I'm honest, it's kind of nice to hear people say flattering things about me. I like the "likes."

Are you catching the problem here? It's all about me. Me, myself, and I, front and center, trying to make a big splash in the body image pool. That's vanity.

> *For am I now seeking the approval of man, or of God? Or am I trying to please man? If I were still trying to please man, I would not be a servant of Christ.* (Galatians 1:10)

I'm guiltily confessing to you that vanity almost stopped me from a video shoot I was planning to record. I was on the brink of *not* recording at all. Why? Because I was heavier than when I made my last video series. And it was, honestly, kind of embarrassing to think about how I'd touted the fact that I'd "changed my metabolism." Yet here I was, in my midforties, battling my metabolism again.

The scale was only up a few pounds. My normal flux puts me at four to six pounds heavier than the last time I was on camera. If you were to watch the videos, you may or may not even notice, but *I* can tell. I even went so far as to sit down on the morning of my scheduled shoot and write out all the other ways I could be helpful to people and provide the same information *without* doing the videos. Know what? It was 100 percent vanity screaming at me. I didn't want to get behind the camera again. I didn't want to talk about health and wellness when I didn't feel like I was at my "best." When I looked in the mirror, I expected to see the lighter, younger, better me. All I could see were flaws.

I needed a haircut.
I needed foils—the gray was taking over.
I needed to tone my arms again.
I needed to lose an inch or two in my belly.
I needed to tackle my skin breakouts.

It all grabbed me, and it grabbed me hard. I felt the shame creeping in right alongside the blame. But I had a single moment of clarity. I thought about all the people I've coached over the years and all the things I've told them. Things like:

"There's perfect eating, and then there's real life."

"Aim for good enough, not perfection."

"Even when you slip, you're not as far back as you once were."

"Just keep swimming."

Was I willing to listen to my own voice, my own message of hope and encouragement to others? Was I willing to follow what I truly believe to my core? I sheepishly said yes to the voice of truth in my head. Sometimes I need that reminder and reset. I need to see through the fog. Can you relate?

In the world of fitness and nutrition, there's constant pressure to be a shining example of everything I preach, and that's hard sometimes. If I'm honest, it's hard most days, and I struggle with feelings of fraud and inadequacy. I am not a great cook. I'm a basic, simple-food-prep kind of gal and not one to count on for great recipes or creative pairings. I microwave vegetables, make tacos about once a week, and often underseason and overcook my chicken. The truth is, I love pizza. I love coffee with cream. I love apple pie and cheesecake. I love a great bacon cheeseburger and pumpkin muffins in the fall.

And I don't like working out. I don't move enough during the day and rarely hit ten thousand steps. But I commit to exercise anyway, about five days a week, because my body is better for it. I'm just a girl trying to outwit (or at least keep up with) an aging metabolism. Real life.

When the focus of my health quest becomes about positive feedback and endorsements, I know it's time for a reset. Appearance—and appearances—should never trump health. When I spend more time working out, thinking about food, or posting on social media than I do in the Word of God, I'm all out of whack. I'm living in the morning fog.

This book is the by-product of a lifetime of accumulated knowledge and wisdom. It's a compilation of messages, notes, and inspiration that I've heard in church for several years. It's recollections from years of growing up in church, obtaining a Bible degree from a Christian college, serving in Bible study leadership, and engaging in conversations with other Christian friends and mentors. I wish I could say more of it has come from intentional, daily time with God. I can't.

Now hopefully I didn't lose too many of you here. I hope I didn't lose my credibility or your confidence that the words on the pages of this book can help you down the path to a healthier life. Instead, I hope I'm connecting with your heart that's maybe feeling the little sting of conviction and resonance.

This chapter evolved after a conversation with a dear friend about this very thing. She's another Christian woman who wonders sometimes if her focus on healthy activities, like exercise and nutrition, captures too much of her time and energy. We shared the same concern and agreed to hold each other accountable in our shared struggle. Additionally, I confessed to one of my frequent hang-ups that some days I get almost paralyzed, and certainly distracted, about whether what I do for "work" matters at all. I deliberate about whether my focus on helping people eat and move better makes any difference at all in the big picture. My mind churns with questions of significance.

> *Wouldn't working in a church (which is why I thought God was leading us to the East Coast) be a better use of my time?*

IT BEGAN IN THE GARDEN

Wouldn't I have more influence there?

Isn't ensuring that people know and love God with all their hearts, strengths, and minds more important than talking to people about food and exercise?

In these questions of doubt, however, I'm drawn gently back to why better food and exercise choices matter. God brings something, or someone, to mind who reinforces the importance of living a healthier life. I'm reminded of a friend whose life was lost, in part, to an unhealthy relationship with food and exercise. I watch people I love struggle with health problems that are aggravated by extra pounds that their bodies aren't intended to carry. I listen to clients share their battles with fatigue, depression, or daunting medical diagnoses. I see lives that are impeded by lack of energy or disease. I see lost legacies.

That's when I know my message matters. *That's* what helps the work I do feel more significant. That's why this book matters. It's my opportunity to coach transformation, which I believe is God's unique purpose for me. Recognizing this greater purpose is what brings everything back into focus. The reflection in that mirror rights itself once again.

Early in the Genesis story, we get a glimpse of God's vision.

So God created human beings in his own image. In the image of God he created them; male and female he created them. (Genesis 1:27)

I'm reminded of a song my husband, Kevin, sang to me on our wedding day. The lyrics from Steven Curtis Chapman's "I Will Be Here" still make me teary and give me goose bumps:

*I will be here, to watch you grow in beauty and
tell you all the things you are to me, I will be here.*

The beauty spoken about here is not physical beauty. Trust
me. I am more wrinkled, gray, and "unevenly distributed"
than I was on my wedding day in 1992. I have battle scars
from a C-section, cyst removals, and plantar warts. Too
much information? It's the truth. It's not always pretty.

Eve was deceived by physical beauty.

> *The woman was convinced. She saw that the
> tree was beautiful and its fruit looked delicious,
> and she wanted the wisdom it would give her.
> So she took some of the fruit and ate it. Then
> she gave some to her husband, who was with
> her, and he ate it, too.* (Genesis 3:6)

The pursuit of a beautiful object led to a bad, and life-
altering, decision. Physical beauty draws us in and
captivates us, but it can lead us to unwise choices and
skewed priorities if we're not careful. Whether it's our own
beauty or someone (or something) else's that intrigues
us, it's never permanent and so very temporal, like the
morning fog. Outward appearances never tell us what's
inside the packaging, buried under the fig leaves. Eve
learned that lesson when she bit into that piece of fruit.
What appeared to be beautiful and pleasing on the surface
was the bitterest bite of food she would ever eat.

There's a term used in the health industry called *skinny
fat.* Though not a technical term, it essentially describes
people who look healthy on the outside but whose vital
statistics tell a different story. As a nutrition coach at a
health club, I found that it was surprisingly common. I met
many club members who appeared fit, even skinny. They
were not visually obese or even overweight. But when
we'd do their blood work, a different story emerged. Their

cholesterol, blood sugar, and triglyceride (how much fat is in the blood) levels showed elevations. The readings would tell an unhealthy story. These visually healthy people were on the verge of serious diseases like insulin resistance, diabetes, or heart disease. Looks are deceiving.

A few years ago, I was on a train headed into Boston. At each stop, more and more passengers made their way into the ever-tightening train car. About halfway into town, a visibly heavy woman boarded the car, looked me straight in the eye, and said in a snarky tone, "You *clearly* don't need to be sitting there." Stunned at first, I realized I was inadvertently sitting in a seat reserved for people with disabilities. I stood and gave up my seat for her. But the longer I was on that train, the more peeved I got. Why? I was feeling judged. This woman decided that, because I was smaller than she was, there was nothing wrong with me. She made a quick assessment that because of my smaller frame, my visual appearance, I did not qualify for that seat.

Now, the truth is, I *didn't* belong in that seat, but *she* didn't know that. She didn't know me at all. I could have had a medical issue or condition that wasn't visually detectable that would have given me a reason to be in that seat. But in one quick glance, she decided I was healthy. Outward appearances open doors, and they sometimes close them.

What if that single piece of fruit hanging from the Garden tree were bruised? What if it had had wormholes and spots? What if it were lopsided? What if it were imperfect? Would Eve have been as enticed?

After Eve ate the apple, she had the same kind of negative reaction that we often do when we see ourselves in the mirror with the light on. I don't know what she saw in her physical appearance when her eyes were opened and she saw herself fully. She had already been stamped "Grade A perfect" by God, her Creator, but when her own physical appearance was revealed, she was seduced with self-consciousness and shame. Somehow her vision of her own body changed when she could see it in the light.

In the end, our ultimate reason for pursuing a life of health and wellness should be for the pursuit of life beyond the scale or mirror. We should focus far more on what we can *do* and who we can *be* when our movements are not encumbered by our weight. Our productivity increases when we have more energy from nutrient-dense food and when we are more engaged in day-to-day life.

Good nutrition and exercise is about so much more than what we look like. The importance of body care transcends physical appearance. It signifies far more than what the mirror and scale show on a given day. The food and exercise choices we make are about the quality of our individual lives and our ability to impact others' lives, too. Our first mission on earth is to share the message of the Bible. When we have energy and strong bodies, we can more fully live out our purpose during our years on earth.

Ultimately, each of our lives will come to an end. We have a start date and an end date. Between those dates is the dash called life. As we live out our dash, we have the opportunity, and responsibility, to impact other people's lives, too. With well-balanced nutrition and more regular movement in our day, we will find ourselves happier, more content, and more aware of the things we are capable of than we are when we're fatigued, lethargic, and depressed.

Here are three non-scale, non-mirror benefits to being healthy:

Nutrition education and awareness.

When we take an interest in food, we start to make better choices. Naturally. We start to realize how much sugar sneaks into our diet, how much protein we really need, or how much we lack veggies and fruits. We learn principles that will carry us into the rest of our lives, regardless of what the scale reads on a given day. It's amazing how quickly our bodies adapt to, and crave, real food. When we go "off the ranch" at a weekend birthday party or a dinner out, we will start to notice how terrible we feel afterward. Experiencing firsthand how food feels in our bodies, both positively (increased energy, improved digestion) and negatively (stomach distress, energy slumps, moods) is crucial to making better food choices for life.

Stronger body for the long haul.
Physical activity that builds our core, back, leg, or arm strength improves our quality of life. The goal isn't to develop a perfect physique or bulging biceps. That's focusing on the fog. Rather, we need to improve our functional fitness as we age so that we can pick things up off the floor, lift a box from our car, or sit cross-legged on the floor with our kids (or grandkids!). There's personal satisfaction in feeling stronger and noticing it in our day to day movements.

Self-confidence and emotional strength.
More than great before-and-after pictures, I am inspired by stories of improved self-belief and confidence. Watching the body language and words change from "I'm not sure I can" to "I know I can" is my biggest payoff as a coach. Feeling in control of food choices, believing a physical challenge is conquerable, and moving with confidence wherever you go is greater than any scale reading, pant size, or mirrored reflection.

It's great to be inspired and motivated by athletic physiques. And it's perfectly okay to feel good about the way you look when you've worked hard to stay fit and healthy. The caution is simply to keep the right perspective and balance in that pursuit. Make sure you're seeing beyond the fog and into the eyes of the only reflection that lasts.

Now we see things imperfectly, like puzzling reflections in a mirror, but then we will see everything with perfect clarity. All that I know now is partial and incomplete, but then I will know everything completely, just as God now knows me completely.
—1 Corinthians 13:12

LESSON 10:
SOLITUDE IS NOT AN OPTION

Moving to a new town is hard, especially when it's in another state, halfway across the country. Though I was a veteran of relocations, having done so five times in my childhood years, our move to New England in 2010 was the first time I'd done so as a parent. This time, instead of being the child who was at the mercy of a parental decision, *I* was the one tearing my boys away from their friends, home, and church. Drew, who was in seventh grade at the time, took it the hardest when we shared our plans. He sobbed while we held him in our living room.

Our first year on the south shore of Boston was filled with hope. We were optimistic about finding a new church home, great friends, and good extracurricular activities for the boys. (We asked *every* realtor about their town's hockey programs!) Yes, there were adjustments with two boys in middle school and one in elementary school, but the overall pace of life had slowed to a nice speed. But life changed in year two. The novelty wore off, and we were worn out. We hadn't found much of what we'd been searching for with church, friends, or sports. And I was lonely.

Life wasn't bad. It was just hard, and it got even harder for a few years. We had two boys in counseling with anxiety issues. I had my own meltdowns in coffee shops and in my closet sobbing that I wanted to go "home." My relationship with Kevin was strained due to my discontent and his self-imposed guilt about being the cause. It's been a rough road sometimes. But ultimately, almost seven years later, we are tighter and closer as a family than we ever would have been if we had stayed in the comfort of the Saint Paul suburbs. What could have torn us apart, and felt like it might at times, brought us together as a family unit stronger than ever. Not perfect but united.

We are created for relationships. It's part of the original Garden masterplan. In the designing and planting in Genesis, God only saw one problem with his work. Almost all of his handiwork was *awesome*. Every living creature was given breath, and the earth was given its awe and wonder. But when God looked around after creating Adam, something was missing. Some*one* was missing. A partner, a companion with whom to share stewardship of everything else he created.

In all that he deemed "good," this one thing was not.

Then the Lord God said, "It is not good for the man to be alone. I will make a helper who is just right for him."

So the Lord God formed from the ground all the wild animals and all the birds of the sky. He brought them to the man to see what he would call them, and the man chose a name for each one. He gave names to all the livestock, all the birds of the sky, and all the wild animals. But still there was no helper just right for him.

So the Lord God caused the man to fall into a deep sleep. While the man slept, the Lord God took out one of the man's rib and closed up the opening. Then the Lord God made a woman from the rib, and he brought her to the man.

"At last!" the man exclaimed.
"This one is bone from my bone,
and flesh from my flesh!

She will be called 'woman,' because she was taken from 'man.'" This explains why a man leaves his father and mother and is joined to his wife, and the two are united into one.
(Genesis 2:18–24)

Perfection! Together they would tend the earth, savor the food, and enjoy the views. Together they would discover each other in every way and produce offspring to populate the earth. Together they would help each other with work, child-rearing, and self-discovery. At least that was the plan. The blueprint. God's ideal. He designed them for relationship. He wanted a connection with Himself first and with others second. Vertical and horizontal relationships. Nothing has changed today. It was his original intent, and it remains so.

When life gets hard, which it often does, we are designed to rely on these relationships for help. God first. People second. In many ways, people are just an extension of him anyway. (Remember that "created in his image" thing?) Without God in the flesh still walking around here on earth, he gives us his hands and feet through other people.

The picture that comes to mind when I think about us being hands and feet for each other is the vision and words of my then four-year-old son, Kyle, during a snowboarding outing with friends. After a wipeout on the "slopes" (a hill at our local golf course), Kyle came to a stop with his head facing down the hill and his snowboard, still attached to his feet, resting higher up the hill. After lying there for a bit, he called out to anyone within earshot, "Um, a little help here?"

Kyle was stuck. Without help, he couldn't get himself out of the crazy position he was in. He had to rely on someone, *anyone*, else to get him moving in the right direction again. He needed my feet to move toward him and my hands to help him get upright. He asked for help.

So many of us try to bare-knuckle it through life. We try to be self-sufficient and strong. In all honesty, we act like toddlers who demand to "do it myself!" But that's not God's plan. He saw Adam's solitude in the garden, and he fixed it. He fixes it for us, too. But we must let him.

Sometimes it takes hitting rock bottom to finally acknowledge that "alone" is not the right solution. In my late thirties, before our move to Massachusetts, I sat in a counseling office waiting room feeling broken, embarrassed, and vulnerable. After years of being the caregiver, I finally acknowledged that I needed to sit in the other chair. I needed help.

The moment of clarity came in the middle of a concert in an auditorium chock-full of people. As I sat in the arena with thousands of others and my husband beside me, I felt completely alone. I sobbed through most of the concert. I knew I was in a big, big hole and couldn't get out of it on my own. My smallness and God's immensity overwhelmed me. I didn't know exactly what was wrong, but I knew I couldn't stay in that place anymore. I needed help, so I entered the counseling office.

Later that day with my appointment behind me, I expressed to a friend how weak I felt sitting in that waiting room. How incapable and even ashamed I felt. She had a different perspective, however. She believed the people in that waiting room were strong. In fact, she believed they were the strongest people she knew. That included me.

She reminded me that it took strength, not weakness, to sit there acknowledging the need for help. She was right.

The bravest people on earth are the ones who acknowledge their brokenness, reach out, and seek help. They are the ones who take steps to reconnect to people who are meant to love us and care for us. It's exponentially harder to ask for help and act on it than it is to continue doing nothing. It's crazy hard. Take it from one who's been there. I thought that whatever I was facing would be a quick fix. A few sessions talking things out and then I'd be on my way, fixed and healed. But I spent the next year meeting with my counselor regularly, working through life together. Those sessions were hard—sometimes really hard—but they helped me heal and move forward. Without those invested hours of counseling, I would likely still be stuck. I *know* I would still be stuck . . . and weak.

Have you been there? Have you felt like you hit rock bottom? Have you felt completely alone, helpless, or without answers? Are you there today? In that moment, you are poised for your greatest display of strength. There are people surrounding you who can help. It's what they were made to do and who they were made to be. They are the hands and feet of Jesus. Christ *is* enough and he *is* all we need. But sometimes we need to experience him with skin on in a flesh-covered body listening, supporting, encouraging, and even challenging us. Our battle for mental and physical health can't be fought alone.

Remember when I ordered that fitness DVD? I knew my chances of success would be so much greater if I brought someone alongside me. I needed some extra hands and feet to help me get through it. My husband was the perfect fit, though some special arrangements had to be made to make this an even better fit. We couldn't actually *do* the workouts together. We couldn't share workout space at the same time. It was all my fault.

Before starting this program, we did our initial fitness testing together. That's when I discovered that he's a shaker. Can you picture it? Every push-up resulted in quivering biceps and legs. Every pull-up amplified the shaking. What can I say? I was a goner. I laughed. He didn't. His normally calm demeanor disappeared as I was doubled over in laughter. It was clear that this was not going to be a good arrangement going forward. So we followed the workout schedule faithfully but did the workouts separately. It worked for us.

We both reached our goals. We had the accountability of knowing the other was pushing Play on the same DVD player on the same schedule. We ate the recommended foods and tracked our progress together. In the evenings, we commiserated. We shared how sore we were, which workouts we liked and didn't, how corny the trainer's jokes were (but how we still liked him), and how tired we were of eating protein, protein, and more protein—especially chicken. We even bonded over a verse in Proverbs that still makes us smile:

> A bowl of vegetables with someone you love
> is better than steak with someone you hate.
> (Proverbs 15:17)

In the end, we celebrated together. We sat across the table from each other at a restaurant and decided right then and there what we wanted to stick with and what we wanted to stop doing.

That experience changed our lives forever. It's been almost eight years since we undertook that challenge together, but we still point to that experience as the turning point for our health. The most important thing we've done for all these years now is to *continue* to hold each other accountable for our health. We've continued to work out at home together . . . but separately! Sometimes we do programs that aren't our personal favorites just to support the other one's choice. We continue to talk about food choices and share when we're feeling a bit off track. The truth is, without the two of us in the same house working toward the same goal, neither of us would be where we are today. We are reliant on the other for accountability, motivation, encouragement, and success.

Community is essential. It's God's design on purpose. We need each other as the body needs its members to function properly. Each member is different but essential, and the diversity of each one is a gift to the others. Yes, Kevin and I are individually responsible for working out, even when we don't want to (and for Kevin, that's very, very early) and we make our own choices about what to eat during the day since dinner is our only shared meal. But if either of us threw in the towel, it would be a whole lot less fun, and we'd be a whole lot less healthy. We are the skin on Jesus for each other.

If you are struggling to stay on track with your nutrition or fitness, one of the very best things you can do is find an accountability partner. If you have a spouse or even a son or daughter who lives in the house with you, I'd strongly encourage you to partner with him or her in your quest for health improvements. The clients I've seen who have been the most successful have a strong support system in place. People who know them, love them, and want to see them succeed.

If you have people in your life who constantly sabotage you or choose not to pursue the same healthy lifestyle as you, you are far less likely to establish a pattern of success. You are not as likely to eat a salad when everyone else is eating pizza. You're not going to say no to dessert if your kids are breaking out the ice cream and cookies.

Recruit your family members to make some healthy changes with you. The less of a big deal you make it, the better. Share some of the things you've learned from this book. Have them participate in the conversation and the processing with you. Choose your words wisely. Take care in how you talk about your body (positively or negatively), and use words that express why you want to make changes for your health, not necessarily how your body looks. Your kids are watching—and listening. If you're constantly talking about being on a diet or referring to yourself as fat or putting yourself down, your kids will start applying the same behaviors and belief systems to themselves. Even boys.

We learned the hard way that our constant dialogue about weight and food and exercise was being heard and internalized by our youngest, Kyle. When he was only nine years old, he casually mentioned one day that he thought he needed to lose weight. Yikes.

I realized that as we sat at the dinner table each night talking about food and fitness, Kyle was absorbing it all. He was internalizing our words and making his own judgments about his body—and ours. He noticed that his two brothers had body types that were different from his own. (Flashback to when I compared *my* body to my mom's and sister's bodies at the same age.) The truth is, they *are* different. One of his brothers requires a belt to hold up his pants thanks to his thin frame. Even slim-fit pants were often too big on him as a young boy, and he still requires slim-cut jeans and khakis as a college student. And the other brother has been referred to by Kyle as a "male model" because of the physique he's worked hard to build. (I can't help but picture Ben Stiller in *Zoolander* right about now!)

Kyle's body has always been different. Though his height and weight have always been within an appropriate range, he's often been a size or two ahead of his brothers at the same age. Kind of ironic given that he was my "small" baby! But in our home, where body-based topics were common, he was absorbing and hearing things through his own filter. Not good.

We needed that wake-up call. It forced us to change our conversations. We talk about health, not weight loss. We talk about making choices and swaps with foods rather than eliminating "bad" foods. Now, as a young teen, he's growing rapidly and his body is changing daily. He has surpassed me in height, making me officially the shortest member of our family now.

Our homes should be a safe place to have healthy conversations. Ideally, your household is a great place for support, too. I realize, however, that not everyone will find it there. Sometimes it's the least healthy place to be. If this describes your situation, reach out to a friend who knows and loves you. Ask your friend to meet you at the gym or go for a walk. Recruit your friend to watch a great nutrition video with you or to keep you accountable for eating your fruits and veggies, or hire a coach. There are so many people, including me, who make it their profession to help you get and stay healthier. I promise you, we rarely do it for the money! If you ask a personal trainer or nutrition coach why they do what they do, without hesitation most will say, "To help people."

New York Times best-selling author Chalene Johnson is a lifestyle and business expert and a motivational speaker. She may be best known as the creator and instructor of many fitness infomercials and workout videos. Her vast experience has led her to the importance of accountability this way:

> You're far more likely to adhere to your habits when you create a fortress of accountability

around them. And the strongest form of accountability comes from outside ourselves.[13]

There are people in your life who want to carry you—family, friends, coaches. You don't have to be married to find a great accountability partner.

Here are three ways to find your strength-building partner:

Acknowledge your challenge.

Living in denial is counterproductive to a life of health. We all struggle. We all have our thorns. When we let go of our pride (i.e., realize that sometimes the caregiver needs to be the care-receiver), the biggest hurdle is already overcome. Pray and ask for help from the One who can provide the ultimate healing. He already knows the struggle but still wants to hear you articulate it to him. He's waiting for you to humble yourself in this way. If you need a boost in your physical health, admit it and submit it to him. No, he's not going to do the work *for* you, but he can provide the human hands, feet, and words to guide you through day-to-day life. God will provide when you are weak.

Tell someone.

The more silent we remain, the more power that "thing" has over us. Sharing is hard, but it's also the bravest thing you'll do. Most likely, your friends and family will welcome the opportunity to pray for you, talk with you, and encourage you. Find a skin on Jesus to support you and walk through your days with you as you build your strength. Remember, we were made to comfort one another and take solace in the shared experiences. We need to feel arms wrapped around us, hear a voice of encouragement and empathy, and simply feel another person's presence even in the silence. And we need those same people to walk, run, and yoga with us in day-to-day life.

Seek professional guidance.

Sometimes we need an expert to walk the road with us. I expected to touch base with a counselor for a month or two. It was almost a year of biweekly sessions. Without her guidance, I would not have moved past the obstacles blocking my life's path. Check with your church or a local organization that's partnered with trusted counselors. The expertise they bring and the truth they speak into your life is life-changing. Even healthy people need a checkup from time to time. And even fitness experts need trainers and coaches.

Consider the familiar words of this childhood Sunday school song:

> *Jesus loves me, this I know. For the Bible tells me so. Little ones to him belong. They are weak but he is strong.*

In our moments of greatest weakness, greatest vulnerability, he gives us strength. His strength makes us strong. Whether you're discouraged by your current health status, job situation, or other life stressor, you are ready for a great opportunity. You are poised for strength. Are you ready to flex?

> *A person standing alone can be attacked and defeated, but two can stand back-to-back and conquer. Three are even better, for a triple-braided cord is not easily broken.*
> —Ecclesiastes 4:12

WE ARE WHO WE THINK

I'd like to believe that Steve Jobs named his groundbreaking computer company *Apple* because it had a little something to do with it being the "first" of its kind. In truth, he reveals in his autobiography that he was on "one of many fruitarian diets and had just come back from an apple farm, and thought the name sounded fun, spirited, and not intimidating."[14] So much for a nice analogy! As for the fruitarian diet? I'll let that one be for now. I do find it intriguing, however, that Apple's slogan is "Think different."

Returning to the story in the Garden of Eden, recall that our image was designed as a reflection of God's.

> *So God created human beings in his own image.*
> *In the image of God he created them; male and*
> *female he created them.* (Genesis 1:27)

When we read this verse, I think we are drawn first to the visual imagery—the body. The word *image* brings with it a visual. A picture. We've talked about this likeness to him in previous lessons in this book. Sometimes we forget, though, that the "made in his likeness" part includes the wholeness of our being—mind, body, and spirit. Adam was gifted with the capacity to use his mind by applying wisdom and knowledge. Pastor Don Fortner suggests this about God's initial design for his people:

> The image of God in which man was created is also reflected in his mental capacity. Like his Creator, Adam was wise, rational, and full of knowledge. He named all living things. He knew his wife when she was brought to him. He knew both good and evil. Though, like Christ himself, before the fall, Adam knew no sin by experience, he knew the nature of it. He knew that it was contrary to God's Being. And he knew the consequences of it.[15]

In short, we were given strong minds that could think, reason, decide, and know right from wrong. Though our judgment and wisdom was clouded by the apple-biting of Adam and Eve, we can reclaim what was lost. We begin to transition out of the old story and into the rest of the story, more of the good news, through the birth and death of Jesus Christ. In him, we can be restored to a place of emotional, physical, and spiritual health.

> *For the sin of this one man, Adam, caused death to rule over many. But even greater is God's wonderful grace and his gift of righteousness, for all who receive it will live in triumph over sin and death through this one man, Jesus Christ.*
> (Romans 5:17)

We *can* be made right again. Through a relationship with Christ, by getting to know him personally, we can be renewed and move closer to the image God intended. We can "think different."

Are *you* ready to think differently? More importantly, do you believe you can? What you believe about your ability to change your story makes all the difference. The script you've written in your head to this point will determine your ability to truly make changes going forward. Simply having the desire to change isn't enough. Being motivated to change isn't enough. You must *believe* you can change for the change to take hold. The script writing begins in your mind.

We've spent years writing our story. Every life experience, every thought, every behavior has built a neural pathway, an actual groove in our brain, that impacts the decisions we make every day. At some point, these grooves automate themselves. We're no longer consciously aware of our thoughts or behaviors. Researcher Wendy Wood studied human behavior and concluded that 40–45 percent of everything we do is a habit.[16] In other words, it's unconscious. We do it automatically.

This is both good and bad. If the things we do automatically take us to a better state of health, like eating a salad for lunch, stopping at the gym on our way home from work, or getting seven or eight hours of sleep every night, then we're likely grateful for this routine. If, however, our robotic behaviors include things like stopping by the vending machine for a midafternoon snack, driving past the gym, or watching late-night television, these patterns are not serving us well.

Becoming more aware, more conscious, of our choices is step one to using the power of habits to our advantage. We need to start *thinking* about our decisions, our behaviors, and our thoughts to begin the process of changing them. The wonderful thing about the brain is that it has a great deal of plasticity, meaning it can change. It's never too late. We are never stuck with the thoughts and patterns, the story, we've constructed. We can build new grooves, new thoughts, new behaviors. We find support for this truth in the book of Romans:

> *Don't copy the behavior and customs of this world, but let God transform you into a new person by changing the way you think. Then you will learn to know God's will for you, which is good and pleasing and perfect.* (Romans 12:2)

The Bible highlights our ability to change the way we think, to renew and transform our minds to make choices that are in keeping with his ideal will and plan for our lives and our bodies.

So, I ask again: What do you believe? What do you believe is "true" about yourself, your body, and your relationship with food? The simplicity of it all is that what we tell ourselves is either a truth or a lie. We listen to the truth of God and what he tells us about who we are—*God created mankind in his own image, in the image of God he created them* (Genesis 1:27)—or we are deceived by the hiss of that darn snake. What do these lies look like? Here are a few:

> *I will never be able to lose weight. I've done this so many times before and failed.*
>
> *If I lose the weight, then I will finally be happy.*
>
> *That person has it all together. If I could just look like her, my life would be perfect.*
>
> *I will never be able to get a handle on my cravings. I'm too weak.*
>
> *I have no self-control or willpower.*
>
> *No one will love me like this.*

Do you recognize these statements? More importantly, are you aware of them? They are lies. Every single one. We feed ourselves truths and lies. The script we tell ourselves, the words we nourish ourselves with, are just as important, if not more so, than the actual food we put into our bodies. If we live on a constant diet of mistruths and self-deprecating beliefs, we are much more likely to have an unhealthy thought life and an unhealthy mind. The broken record continues to play the warped song. On the other hand, if we feed our minds life-giving, nourishing statements, we affirm our identities and health in Christ.

Think about the things you tell yourself in daily life. What are the first words that come to mind when you look in the mirror? What do you tell yourself when you eat that doughnut or fast-food hamburger? Do you know? Have you listened? Now consider this: Would you say those same words out loud to a friend? How about to your child? If your answer is no, then why are you saying them to yourself?

I became aware of my own thought patterns recently as the scale started to creep up again. I was in a bad place of berating myself for my lack of self-control and discipline. I looked in the mirror—at my thighs, of course—and looked away in disgust. I caught myself squeezing the little extra, the muffin top, that was squirting out the top of my jeans (when I wasn't wearing workout pants). And I was really frustrated when my favorite jeans didn't fit at all.

By divine intervention, I was listening to a podcast in my car. Now, I haven't listened to *anything* in my car for years— no music, no talk radio, no podcasts. Just silence. But that day I felt prompted to listen to an audio recording distributed by the Institute for the Psychology of Eating. In truth, it was an unwanted freebie I'd gotten with the purchase of a book, but with a forty-minute drive ahead of me, I pressed Play on the recording. And the heavens parted (at least that's the way it felt). The words that followed were exactly what I needed to hear at exactly the right moment. God used a human messenger to speak to me.

I was encouraged to think about my own history with food and my body. And for the first time, I realized that I was telling myself a whole lot of lies. I was feeding myself with self-loathing, harshness, and negativity. I was squeezing out truths to make room for Satan's subtle deceptions. I was pushing love and grace to the side. I was at war with my body and spirit. And it started in my mind.

This wake-up call, this awareness, led me to make two changes. First, I stopped getting on the scale in the morning. I realized that I started writing a bad story from the second I woke up by allowing a number to dictate how I felt about myself. That simple reading determined the entire trajectory of my day. My mood, my food choices, and my self-talk. Secondly, I pulled one truth from Scripture and recited it every time I looked in the mirror. Whether fully clothed or completely naked, I started repeating these words, "I am fearfully and wonderfully made."

A funny thing happened. I started smiling more at myself, at my true reflection. Sometimes, I even laughed—even when my zipper didn't close, even when my muffin top rolled out, even when my hair wasn't cooperating. I felt joy for the first time in a long time. That's a pretty big deal for me, a woman whose struggle with depression and anxiety is very real.

Science has recently proven what the Bible has always said is true; joy is the best motivator for lasting change. We are much more likely to make positive changes to our behavior out of a place of joy versus a place of fear. A sobering study at Johns Hopkins University followed bypass surgery patients post-op. When confronted with the fact that they could prevent the need for additional surgery or even death by making healthy life changes, 90 percent of them didn't change their lifestyles.[17] Clearly, fear is *not* the primary motivator for decision-making, even when death is on the line. (Remember Adam and Eve's decision?)

The biggest discovery in this study is that joy is the most important motivator for any real and lasting change. Our emotions do, in fact, play an integral part in our ability to make lasting changes. By experiencing more joy and being in a good place emotionally, we consciously write a better story, one that does not allow a negative script to dominate our lives. When you're battling your own emotions and fearing you'll lose the battle, remember who the *real* enemy is.

> *Stay alert! Watch out for your great enemy, the devil. He prowls around a roaring lion looking for someone to devour.* (1 Peter 5:8)

You have a very real enemy who's planting deceptions and falsehoods in your mind and heart. He's relying on you to become numb with his whispers and to fall into an unconscious trance with his hiss. He's counting on his self-talk becoming your self-talk. He's hungry for you.

If you have any competitive bone in your body, stand up and fight! Declare truth to yourself. Feed yourself words of love and kindness. Envelop yourself with a nice, warm cotton blanket instead of the holey fig-leaf kind. Claim victory and joy.

> *Don't let my enemies gloat, saying, "We have defeated him!" Don't let them rejoice at my downfall. But I trust in your unfailing love. I will rejoice because you have rescued me. I will sing to the Lord because he is good to me.* (Psalms 13:4–6)

Satan doesn't have to win. He doesn't have to rejoice at your demise or lick his lips in anticipation of the subtle (or not-so-subtle) ways he's ready to devour you. He knows our eternity is at stake.

Here are three ways you can win the battle for your mind:

Tune back in.

Pay attention to the dialogue in your head. What messages do you tell yourself when you look in the mirror, sit down to eat, or go to bed at night? What do you feel because of those thoughts? A simple way to diagnose whether these are truths or lies is to ask yourself, "Do those thoughts take me closer to or further away from God?" If you feel the need to run and hide from him, it's pretty fair to say the lies are winning. But if you feel the smallest inkling of hope, joy, and peace, you are living a healthier, more truth-filled script. Just start noticing and naming your daily dialogue. Your inner dialogue is the key to changing your relationship with food and your body.

Claim ownership.

You are a child of God. Whether you've acknowledged that yet or not, he loves you just as you are today, with warts, blemishes, imperfections, cellulite, and all. This is the foundational truth that underwrites your entire life. But you have a choice. You can *live* as though this is truth or not. Believing you are a valued child who is worthy of extravagant love changes everything about how you live today. It doesn't promise a life of perfection, but it does promise that he will be with you every day of your life. Revelation 3:20 promises his companionship: "Look! I stand at the door and knock. If you hear my voice and open the door, I will come in, and we will share a meal together as friends."

Fill it back up.

After we've begun to empty ourselves of the falsehoods that lead to guilt, shame, and regret, we need to replace them with a new identity, a character who's been given a sharp new pencil with which to write a healthier story. Immersion in the Word of God is the very best way to do this. Whether it's reading the Bible, listening to music with faith-based lyrics, or hearing the words spoken by a pastor or Christian leader, the more we fill our minds with truth, the more readily accessible it will be when we need it. We can create new grooves in our brains while the old ones fill in from underuse. This new wiring will become the new and improved habit you've desired for so long.

I'm sure I will step back on the scale again, but not until I can prevent it from robbing my joy. For now, I'm focusing on training my brain to love me just as I am. My body and spirit will follow. I encourage you to do the same brain training. Feed yourself truth today. Renew and transform your mind. For the good of your health, choose joy.

We destroy every proud obstacle that
keeps people from knowing God.
We capture their rebellious thoughts
and teach them to obey Christ.
—2 Corinthians 10:5

LESSON 12:

ENDINGS ARE JUST THE BEGINNING

My boys are back in Minnesota. Well, two of them are as college students at neighboring schools less than three miles apart. They both chose to return to their home state following their graduation from high school five and six years (respectively) after our relocation. Their hearts still pump Minnesota blood.

Though Alex was initially enthusiastic about our move to the East Coast, by the time he was in high school, he couldn't wait to get out of Dodge. He was ready to move on with life. When he was still in middle school, the new high school opened in our town. After touring it with his soon-to-be freshman brother, Drew, he wanted to skip his eighth-grade year so he, too, could be in that new building. He has always preferred to be just one step further into the future. He loves new beginnings.

Do you remember those Choose Your Own Adventure books? They were favorites of mine as a young girl. If you're not familiar with them, they go something like this . . .

The story always starts the same. You start a book with the same characters and the same scenario. At the end of the introduction, however, the characters are faced with a dilemma of some kind and must choose one of two paths.

As the reader, *you* get to decide which choice they make. Your decision prompts you to turn to the appropriate page to read the next part of the story, which prompts another moment of choice. Sometimes the ending is tragic. Literally, the characters will die (fall off a cliff or get eaten by a monster), and the story is over after chapter 1. The end. A single decision leads to a short-lived story. You are startled and surprised that opening a door or choosing a seemingly nonthreatening path leads to death.

Sometimes, however, the characters are taken on a grand adventure. You experience chapter after chapter of mini-adventures. You make many, many choices resulting in better, longer stories and better endings—happily ever after endings.

We are living that same kind of story. Just like those childhood books, the beginning is always the same. The same characters, Adam and Eve, are faced with the same dilemma. We can't change it. Genesis will always read the same, no matter how many times we open its pages. But as the introductory chapters end, we make the next decision. And the next. When the chapter closes on Adam and Eve, it's just our beginning. Though we inherited the start, the rest of the choices are up to us.

I believe what draws readers to the Choose Your Own Adventure books is the abundance of potential. So many possibilities await us. So many different stories can be lived within the pages of the book, and *we* are responsible for the direction. At the end of each page, a new decision awaits. Sometimes our decision leads to a really great chapter. We laugh and run and play and dance. Sometimes it leads to challenges and heartache. We run into a big scary something or fall off a ledge we didn't see coming.

Sometimes a chapter lasts for multiple pages. We're engrossed in the pages and don't want it to end. Sometimes a chapter is very brief. We are grateful when it ends and we can start the story over again.

Sometimes we forget which choice we've made. The story seems familiar, but we just can't recall the outcome. Strangely, we end up repeating a choice that led to the unhappy ending we wanted to avoid this time. We're incredibly adept at forgetting the consequences of our decision, even if we've made it dozens of times.

Sometimes, the pain isn't strong enough to remind us not to do it again. Or maybe the lure of the *hisssssss* is too strong to resist, and we find ourselves giving in to the same temptation that we promised to avoid if faced with it again.

In its simplest form, life is just a series of decisions. We write page after page and learn lesson after lesson until life comes to an inevitable end. And it will come. We're promised that. If you've found that your story has gone a little off track and you've ended up with a story line that's not taking you to a happier ending, you can "right" the story. Author and StoryBrand founder Donald Miller puts it this way:

> By God's design, you are the principal character of your story because you are the only character in any story you can control. You are the storyteller and the principal character all in one. The story may be about something other than you, but you have agency and to deny that is to tell a really boring story. The first of many keys to living a great life is to take full responsibility for our lives.[18]

God has given us authorship. He has given us the gift of choice. We were given free will by a God who loved us enough to give us that responsibility. He knew we would sometimes choose a dangerous path or write a script that would keep us far away from him, yet he still offered this kind of freedom to us. He loved us *that* much.

Adam and Eve wrote a script that led to their deaths and ours, but a loving God had no other choice than to give them that choice. Depending on your theology (which we won't dive into here), we could argue that he knew they'd make that choice, yet he gave them that choice anyway. Sounds kind of crazy, doesn't it? Think about it this way: If he had *not* given them choice, would God be consistent with his character? If first and foremost God is love, how loving would it have been if he had *forced* Adam and Eve to love him? How about if he had created them to live as robots, carrying out his prerecorded script?

Could God have jumped in front of that serpent and stopped Eve from taking a bite of that fruit? Unquestionably, yes. Could he have stopped Adam from following suit and at least salvaged his first original creation? No doubt. Could God do the same for you and me when we are about to do something that's damaging to our health or our lives? Absolutely. But just as with Adam and Eve, the God of love has given us ample warning that there are consequences for our choices. Hasn't He already told us what is and is not beneficial for the sake of a better life?

He told Adam and Eve firsthand. He's told us through his Word, the Bible, and he uses the voice of others, who study it and share it with us, to ingrain it further. We have access to it 24-7. It outlines everything we need for a healthy life. The Bible is our ultimate, highly personalized Choose Your Own Adventure story. Within its pages are story after story with decision-making potential. We read about characters who failed and succeeded. We learn lesson after lesson about men and women of God who were real, flawed, imperfect people with every issue imaginable. We commiserate with Job, celebrate with Abraham, and weep with Mary.

We are equipped to make wise decisions. We are cautioned to avoid sin. We are encouraged to share our faith with others. We are consoled when we face sorrow. We are celebrated when we turn our lives over to Christ. And so much more. As we read, we are encouraged to choose. Ultimately, we have two choices. We can place the book back neatly on the shelf and go about our lives unchanged. We can remain unaffected, or more likely apathetic, in applying the truth we've learned. I admit, I've done it. Or we can take the truth we've read and put it into action. We can right wrongs, seek justice, love mercy, and carry out grace in all things and to all people, including ourselves.

Why does all this matter? You have a unique purpose in this world. You have been equipped to do something that only you can do. It's a purpose only you can fulfill, no one else. If you don't do it, who will? If you're too unhealthy to carry out your God-given purpose, what happens to the people you were intended to help? If you are too unhealthy to play with your grandchildren or read Bible stories to them, what happens to their lives and their children's lives?

Your health, your wellness, will help you live out *your* purpose to its fullest. Compromised health is a barrier, a stumbling block, that trips us up on the way to doing the things God intends for us to do and being the people he wants us to be. We are called to live in a way that honors the one and only body, the temple, we've been given. Good eating and exercise habits build not only a strong physical body but a body that is mentally and emotionally strong as well. We build total health from the inside out. Better health is a side effect of better choices. Weight loss is a side effect of better choices.

The payoff is so much more than that, however. *You* are so much more than that. You are far more than a number on a scale, a pant size, or a perfect photograph. Remember, you are "fearfully and wonderfully made" (Psalms 139:14) by a God who loves you and wants the best for you.

If you're reading this book but have never read the Bible, the Good Book I've been referring to throughout, or you have left it dusty on your shelf for too long, I'd encourage you to start your next chapter there. Pick up a Bible at your local bookstore, order it on Amazon, or borrow one from a local church (most will give them out for free). Dig one out of the attic, or find the one that's buried beneath the other books in your home.

Start at the beginning. Read the Genesis story for yourself with an open heart and a fresh perspective. Learn about the God who made this world and everything in it. Hear and feel his love resonate deep down inside of you and awaken something new. Find hope, and find yourself in the story. You need to know and hear firsthand that you are loved beyond anything you can imagine. You are valued so highly that you are part of a heritage that was given the gift of choice. You are part of a great story. He had you in mind from the very beginning. You, just as you are today, are perfectly imperfect.

God still loved Adam and Eve, even though their choice hurt him, and he still loves us today, unconditionally.

> For this is how God loved the world: He gave his one and only Son, so that everyone who believes in him will not perish but have eternal life. (John 3:16)

God loves this world, and he loves you no matter what choices you've made or are yet to make. His love for you is not what is at stake. That's automatic. The quality and impact of your life is what's at the heart of the quest for healthy living. He promises that if we dive into his Word, seek his wisdom, follow his teachings, and put our trust in him, *then* health will follow.

*My child, never forget the things I have taught
you.*
  Store my commands in your heart.
If you do this, you will live many years,
  and your life will be satisfying.
Never let loyalty and kindness leave you!
  Tie them around your neck as a reminder.
  Write them deep within your heart.
*Then you will find favor with both God and
people,*
  and you will earn a good reputation.
Trust in the Lord with all your heart;
  do not depend on your own understanding.
Seek his will in all you do,
  and he will show you which path to take.
Don't be impressed with your own wisdom.
  Instead, fear the Lord and turn away from evil.
Then you will have healing for your body
  and strength for your bones.
(Proverbs 3:1-8)

Pursue God. Store his commands in your heart. Be loyal and
kind. Trust his guidance for your life. Rely on his wisdom
when you're lacking it. Turn from Satan's temptations. *Then*
you live a long life of true health.

If this sounds like the kind of life you want to live or the
kind of person you want to be, take action! Don't wait. Use
the application points at the end of each chapter. Memorize
the Bible verses. Use the resource section at the end of this
book to help you on the journey. Recruit a friend, team up
with a family member, or hire a coach.

The choice you make today matters. What are you
waiting for? Every page you turn takes you closer to your
final chapter. It's time to choose a better ending.

*"He will wipe every tear from their eyes,
and there will be no more death or
sorrow or crying or pain. All these
things are gone forever."
And the one sitting on the throne said,
"Look, I am making everything new!"
And then he said to me, "Write this
down, for what I tell you is trustworthy
and true."*
—Revelation 21:4–5

ACKNOWLEDGMENTS

First and foremost, this book would not have been possible without the guidance and inspiration of the Holy Spirit. In my weakness, he is strong. He has led and guided me for forty-six years, and he is the reason these words have been written. May my words be light and life and point you back to him.

The primary inspiration for this book came through weekly worship at Grace Church in Avon, Massachusetts, under the teaching of Pastor Sean Sears. His knack for storytelling and unique illustrations lit the spark for this book. I give full credit for the "fig-leaf jacket" inspiration to him.

Additionally, an invaluable part of my faith formation, growth, and spiritual development is because of Eagle Brook Church in the Minneapolis-St. Paul suburbs of Minnesota. All of the speaking pastors have spoken brilliantly into my life and continue to do so thanks to modern technology. Bob Merritt, in particular, has been instrumental in exemplifying the ability to speak hard truth with great love and a bit of humor, too. Thank you for reading an early copy of this book and for providing the foreword.

To my longtime friend and theologian, Jim Beilby, thank you for sharing your wisdom, counsel, honesty, and theological brilliance.

I am exceptionally grateful for the wise female mentors who have fed me biblical wisdom and spiritual truths—Julie Miller, Penny Hegseth, and Jo Rathmanner. Your friendships and guidance have been a crucial part of sharpening my faith.

A special thanks to Margie Broman, whose first glance at the very rough, early chapters of this book provided the breath of life I needed to keep writing. Your tips and encouragement kept me focused for over a year. Cindy Mather, my first editor, was one of your unexpected gifts to me.

To my lifelong friend, Kristi Paulsen, our long-distance phone calls were invaluable in sharpening and honing the message in this book. Lesson 11 is all because of you. God sent me an unexpected gift when he nudged me to share this project with you. Our complementary gifts are an example of God's amazing design and intention for living life in community.

To all the brave souls, past and present, who have shared your stories with me, thank you for sharing your pain, your struggles, and your victories. Please know that on my early-morning drives and in my daily life, I prayed for you. I prayed that I would be of some help to you and that God would infuse my words with his. I hope you heard them. This book is for you.

My first mentor, Wade Wahl, was my college psychology professor, advisor, and friend. He taught me the skill of integrating my faith into daily life and viewing life as an opportunity for careful examination. He modeled integrity, even in the face of adversity, and taught me the value of doing the same. My love for helping people dive into their stories was developed under his guidance. You are greatly missed here on earth to this day. Our loss is heaven's gain.

Wade's colleague Carol Morgan helped me dig into my own messy story when I needed help. Under her care, I healed. She helped me write a healthier future.

To my own coaches, Adam Feit, who walked with me for a year through the completion of my Precision Nutrition Level 2 Certification, and Morgan Rotz, who helped me hone my coaching skills and provided great feedback on this book, you are mentors I now call friends.

To my launch team who helped prepare this book for publication and distribution, thank you for your genuine feedback, honesty, and time supporting me and this book. Thank you for making this "team of one" a team of fifty strong.

To my parents, whose heritage of faith provided the foundation for life, your love and support of me, your tomboy daughter, was invaluable during the crazy adolescent years and remains to this day. You have been my biggest fans and my source of wisdom and stability from the very beginning.

To my sister, who's my very best friend, though we had our early tumultuous years with battles over clothes, differing personalities, and interests, you have been one of my greatest sources of joy. You support me, encourage me, and challenge me, even when it's not easy. Physical distance has never been a barrier to our closeness. Together we are even better.

To my boys, who have provided fodder for this book, thank you for allowing me to share your sometimes less-than-flattering stories on these pages. Despite the yogurt aisle, GameStop, and dinner table squabbles, I couldn't love you more. You have taught me more lessons than could ever be shared in a book. You continue to amaze me with your characters, maturity, wisdom, and love for the Lord. Thank you for proving that my imperfections have led to perfectly wonderful young men.

And to my husband, Kevin, you are my soul mate. You have given me freedom to think, dream, and deliberate, sometimes to the point of exasperation. Your patience and kindness was evident from the day I met you, and I have relied on those qualities for twenty-eight years. You have listened intently, corrected my course with gentleness, and stood by my ever-changing direction time and time again. No matter where the path may lead, as long as I'm with you, it's exactly where I'm meant to be. God's greatest gift to me was you.

READING GUIDE

Lesson 1: Food Fights Are Messy

Think about your own story.

1. What choices have you made that have brought you closer to ideal health?

2. What choices have taken you further away from health?

Use these questions to guide your discovery. Fill in the blanks with as many statements as you'd like:

"When I [blank], I feel healthy."
"When I [blank], I feel unhealthy."

Now, it's time to consider *why* you want to change your health. To do this requires some digging, some deeper gardening. Start by asking yourself this series of questions:

What change do you want to make to your health?
Why is that reason for changing your health important to you?
And why is *that* important?
And what difference will that make?
And why will that previous thing matter?

You've now uncovered the true root, your motivation, for change. Post it where you can read it daily (bathroom mirror, car dashboard, computer screen). Writing down your motivation and desire for a healthier life will keep you moving toward the life you truly want.

Scripture Meditation:

> *For I am about to do something new. See, I have already begun! Do you not see it? I will make a pathway through the wilderness. I will create rivers in the dry wasteland.* (Isaiah 43:19)

Lesson 2: There Will Always Be a Yogurt Aisle

Think about your food choices.

1. What foods do you eat regularly that don't grow from a plant or the earth?

2. What foods do you eat regularly that are a part of a plant-based food or creation?

3. If you were to add a single fruit or vegetable to your day, what would it be?

4. What other fruits and vegetables do you like?

5. What fruit or vegetable would you like to try, either for the first time or for a second chance?

Commit to adding *one* fruit or vegetable to your day. Do an Internet search for a couple of tasty ways to prepare the food of your choice and try the new recipe! Pick the time you want to eat it, and start incorporating that food into a daily meal or snack. Simply adding a single nourishing food to your day can trigger better health.

Scripture Meditation:

> *That is why I tell you not to worry about everyday life —whether you have enough food and drink, or enough clothes to wear. Isn't life more than food, and your body more than clothing?*
> (Matthew 6:25)

Lesson 3: The Devil's Not to Blame

Think about how food makes you feel.

Consider the foods you eat and fill in the blanks:

"When I eat [blank], I feel [blank]."

Spend one day keeping a food journal. I'm not talking about the calorie-tracking kind of journal. Instead, keep a list of the foods you eat and what you are feeling before, during, and after that meal or snack.

Are you angry? Sad? Happy? Excited? Discouraged? Bored?

Now, think back to what happened prior to experiencing that emotion.

1. What happened fifteen minutes before you ate that food?

2. What happened the hour before?

3. What happened two hours before . . . and two hours before . . . and two hours before?

This requires careful observance on your part and a willingness to maybe take on some tough stuff, but the payoff will be better awareness of your emotional state around food, which leads to more intentional eating as a result.

Scripture Meditation:

People who conceal their sins will not prosper, but if they confess and turn from them, they will receive mercy. (Proverbs 28:13)

Lesson 4: Fig-Leaf Jackets Are Holey
Think about your body.

1. What's the first thought that pops into your mind when you picture yourself naked?

2. What body part do you find yourself obsessing about or most self-conscious about?

3. What do you want to hide from everyone, including your spouse?

Call a truce with your body. Begin a daily practice that will help you focus on rebuilding your relationship with your body. Choose one of these ideas, or create your own:

1. Keep a gratitude journal. Start your day by simply writing one sentence about why your body is amazing.

2. Write down ten things you love about your body and post them in a place where you will be reminded about them every day.

3. Choose a friend or family member who will hold you accountable when you make self-deprecating statements. Give him or her permission to call you out when you say something negative about your body.

Do not soft-pedal these self-love statements. No "buts" or "if onlys" or "sort ofs." Go all in! No shame allowed.

Scripture Meditation:

> Thank you for making me so wonderfully complex! Your workmanship is marvelous—how well I know it. (Psalms 139:14)

Lesson 5: God Will Give You More Than You Can Handle

Think about your season of life.

What storm stage are you in today? Are you heading into a storm, in the middle of one, or coming out of one?

Consider these questions based on your answer:

1. What can I personally take responsibility for to make my situation just a little bit better?

2. Is my attitude helping or hurting this situation?

3. How are my food choices impacted by my emotional state?

Planning and preparing is one of the best ways to be ready for whatever life throws at you. Choose one area of your life to "automate" so you don't have to think so much in the midst of stress or an unexpected hiccup in your day. Some examples of this might be:

1. Pick *one* meal or snack to standardize in order to remove decision-making from the equation. Make it the same every day.

2. Pair a new habit (something you want to do regularly) with something you're already doing. For example, pack your lunch/snack when you're already making kids' lunches, or put your multivitamins next to your coffeepot as a reminder to take them.

3. Do five push-ups before you sit on the couch to watch your evening television shows.

You can make small daily, healthy choices, no matter what life throws at you!

Scripture Meditation:

> *Dear friends, don't be surprised at the fiery trials you are going through, as if something strange were happening to you. Instead, be very glad— for these trials make you partners with Christ in his suffering, so that you will have the wonderful joy of seeing his glory when it is revealed to all the world.* (1 Peter 4:12-13)

Lesson 6: Pain in Childbirth Stinks

Think about your daily activity.

How would you identify yourself?

1. Highly active (over ten thousand steps a day, high-intensity exercise, on your feet most of day)

2. Moderately active (around ten thousand steps a day, exercise three or four times per week, combination of sitting and standing)

3. Sedentary (fewer than ten thousand steps a day, no exercise or less than two times per week, mostly seated during the day)

No matter how you identify yourself today, you can use the following principle to make progress toward more regular activity.

Commit to one new activity. Make it easy—really, really easy. For example:

1. Do five daily push-ups.

2. Walk an extra five hundred steps.

3. Take the stairs rather than the elevator at work.

4. Park farther from the entrance to the store.

On a confidence scale of 1–10 (10 being *most* confident ... or 100 percent confident), what number would you give yourself if your goal was to do that activity every day for two to four weeks? If you can't give yourself a 9 or above on that confidence scale, make the activity easier until you can give yourself a 9 or 10.

Think of this as your "ridiculously easy experiment." Now it's time to get going. Start practicing! You are rewiring your brain for success!

Scripture Meditation:

> *She is clothed with strength and dignity, and she laughs without fear of the future. When she speaks, her words are wise, and she gives instructions with kindness. She carefully watches everything in her household and suffers nothing from laziness.* (Proverbs 31:25-27)

Lesson 7: Food Is Not a Moral Issue

Think about your food labels.

No, not the ones on the actual packaging but the ones you've created in your own mind. Take out a piece of paper and make two columns. On one side, list all the foods you'd put in the "bad" category. On the other, list all the foods you'd put in the "good" category.

Now, cross out the words *good* and *bad* at the top of the list. Simply circle the foods that make you feel your best. Choose a food you circled and add it to your daily nutrition at breakfast, lunch, or dinner. Take pleasure in it! Conversely, enjoy a "bad" food but plan for it. There are several ways you can do this:

1. Choose one meal each week to treat yourself. Have pizza or a burger or pie. Look forward to and anticipate it with joy!

2. Choose a daily treat to include in your week. Enjoy a piece of dark chocolate, coffee with cream, or a glass of red wine with dinner. Eat or drink it slowly, savoring the experience.

Aim for eating nourishing foods about 80 percent of the time, but enjoy the 20 percent, too! Consider what works best for you and then build that healthy balance into your week.

Scripture Meditation:

> *That is why I tell you not to worry about everyday life—whether you have enough food and drink, or enough clothes to wear. Isn't life more than food, and your body more than clothing?*
> (Matthew 6:25)

Lesson 8: We Want What We Can't Have

Think about what foods you think you "can't have."

1. Why are they off limits?

2. How do you feel when you eat them, emotionally and physically?

3. How has depriving yourself of certain foods or restricting yourself worked for you in the past?

4. How many times have you lost or gained weight or both through dieting?

To reestablish and balance your relationship with food, for the next two weeks, eat slowly. Slow down. You don't even have to change *what* you eat at all. Just taste your food. Savor it. Notice the flavor, texture, and nuances of it. Spend at least twenty minutes at each meal. Your body will start to tell you what it wants and doesn't want. Your body will naturally tell you what is "off limits" if you just take time to listen to it. This kind of eating will release you from the bondage of food and give you back your freedom!

Scripture Meditation:

> *By his divine power, God has given us everything we need for living a godly life. We have received all of this by coming to know him, the one who called us to himself by means of his marvelous glory and excellence.* (2 Peter 1:3)

Lesson 9: We're Looking at the Wrong Reflection
Think about your *why*.

Go back to lesson 1 and remind yourself why you want to live a healthier life.

1. Is what you're doing today still in keeping with that reason?

2. Have you made progress, or have you gotten distracted?

3. Beyond your physical appearance, what are the additional benefits of eating well or exercising more regularly?

If you've gotten sidetracked, consider taking a break from the scale. If you are doing daily weigh-ins, drop down to once a week or not at all for a season. Though there's benefit to keeping track of ebbs and flows of weight, there are other non-scale methods for tracking your progress. How else can you measure your progress?

1. How do your pants fit?

2. How is your energy level?

3. How are you sleeping?

4. Do you stop eating before you're full?

These progress measures are much better in the long run for both our physical and emotional health. There's no magic number for happiness. Remind yourself it's about wellness, not weight.

Scripture Meditation:

> *Now we see things imperfectly, like puzzling reflections in a mirror, but then we will see everything with perfect clarity. All that I know now is partial and incomplete, but then I will know everything completely, just as God now knows me completely.* (1 Corinthians 13:12)

Lesson 10: Solitude Is Not an Option

Think about your support system.

1. Who's on your side?

2. Who's got your back, no matter what?

3. Who supports, encourages, uplifts, and motivates you?

If you've got a solid system, thank those people! Tell them how much you appreciate them, need them, and count on them for a healthy life.

If you don't have a good support system in place, start building it.

1. Share your health goals with *one* friend or family member and ask that person to hold you accountable and to support you as you work toward your goals.

2. Be specific with your support person. Ask him or her to text you daily or call you weekly.

3. Invite someone to join you a few times a week for a great workout or a nice walk together.

4. Hire a coach, trainer, or counselor. Their passion is to help and support you.

Gradually, you can add more to your network of supporters. The larger your support system, the greater your chance of not only meeting but exceeding your goal. We were never meant to make it on our own.

Scripture Meditation:

> *A person standing alone can be attacked and defeated, but two can stand back-to-back and conquer. Three are even better, for a triple-braided cord is not easily broken. (Ecclesiastes 4:12)*

Lesson 11: We Are Who We Think

Think about your self-dialogue.

1. What negative thought is the most prevalent in your day?

2. When you "mess up," what do you say to yourself?

3. When you are successful, what do you tell yourself?

4. If you were your own best friend, what words of affirmation would you speak to yourself? Start acting as if you are worth it.

Treat yourself like you would treat your child, spouse, or beloved friend.

1. Choose a go-to phrase or verse that you will begin speaking to yourself throughout the day.

2. When you catch yourself glancing in the mirror and casting criticisms on yourself because of the way you look, repeat those positive words to yourself. Say them aloud if that works for you.

Whether spoken in the silence of your own mind or resonated in the space in which you reside, believe that you, just as you are, are fearfully and wonderfully made (Psalms 139:14).

Scripture Meditation:

> *We destroy every proud obstacle that keeps people from knowing God. We capture their rebellious thoughts and teach them to obey Christ.* (2 Corinthians 10:5)

Lesson 12: Endings Are Just the Beginning

Think about your life story.

1. What adventure have you written so far?

2. What stories have you repeated that you'd like to stop before you turn another page?

3. If you were to fast-forward to the end of your life, your final chapter, do you like how your story ends?

It's never easy to think about "the end," but if you've put your faith in Jesus Christ, you have the assurance of knowing what's after the end of your time here on earth. If this describes you, consider how you can use your life for the good of those around you.

1. Is your health helping or hurting the unique purpose you have while you're here?

2. If you were to make healthy changes, what (and who) would benefit?

3. What step can you take today to live more fully—body, mind, and spirit?

If you're unsure about what comes after that final chapter, begin a quest to find out.

1. Open a Bible and start reading the opening chapter in Genesis. Your story began in the Garden.

2. Check out a local church or visit one online.

3. Start a conversation with someone. Encourage him or her to read this book, too, and discuss it together. Question, process, and think together.

As much as it's in your power to do so, write a story that brings you closer to a life of whole-body health. Your body, mind, and spirit are at stake.

Scripture Meditation:

> *He will wipe every tear from their eyes, and there will be no more death or sorrow or crying or pain. All these things are gone forever. And the one sitting on the throne said, "Look, I am making everything new!" And then he said to me, "Write this down, for what I tell you is trustworthy and true."* (Revelation 21:4–5)

ADDITIONAL RESOURCES

As my gift to you for purchasing this book (and reading it to the end!), I have complled additional tools for you to take your next healthy step. The exclusive bonus content includes:

Recipes
Workout Guidance
Nutrition & Supplement Recommendations
Free Books, Videos, and Devotionals
Additional Book Recommendations
Coaching & Counseling Resources

You can find these resources by visiting this link: **www.heidizwart.com/p/garden-book-bonus.**

ENDNOTES

1 Toyota Corporation, "Ask 'why' five times about every matter," http://www.toyota-global.com/company/toyota_traditions/quality/mar_apr_2006.html.

2 Jennifer Dublino, "Scent Marketing for Retailers," http://www.slideshare.net/procreative/retail-and-scent-mktg-13497008.

3 *Financial Perspectives*, "Just for the Smell of It," http://www.financialperspectives.biz/perspectives-investment-blog/ygtxsmb3nrm7nkzcxs6kyykknpczxf.

4 Ryan Andrews, "All About Kitchen Makeovers," http://www.precisionnutrition.com/all-about-kitchen-makeovers.

5 Joe Patrice, "Top 10 Frivolous Lawsuits List Is... Frivolous, But Funny," http://abovethelaw.com/2015/12/top-10-frivolous-lawsuits-list-is-frivolous-but-funny.

6 Quoted in Kenneth Cooper, *Faith-Based Fitness* (Nashville: Nelson, 1995), 25.

7 John Berardi, PhD, "Fitness Success Secrets: On practicing one strategic habit at a time," http://www.precisionnutrition.com/one-habit.

8 Karen Koenig, *The Rules of "Normal" Eating* (Carlsbad, CA: Gurze Books, 2005).

9 Isabel Foxen Duke, "What Does 'Normal' Eating Even Mean?" http://isabelfoxenduke.com/what-does-normal-eating-even-mean-2.

10 Wikipedia, "Stanford marshmallow experiment," https://en.wikipedia.org/wiki/Stanford_marshmallow_experiment.

11 Walter Mischel; Ebbesen, Ebbe B.; Raskoff Zeiss, Antonette, "Cognitive and attentional mechanisms in delay of gratification," *Journal of Personality and Social Psychology*. 21 (2): 204–218.

12 Maia Szalavitz, "The Secrets of Self-Control: The Marshmallow Test 40 Years Later," http://healthland.time.com/2011/09/06/the-secrets-of-self-control-the-marshmallow-test-40-years-later.

13 Chalene Johnson, "7 Day Challenge: Accountability Is Key!" http://www.chalenejohnson.com/7-day-challenge-accountability-is-key/

14 Steve Rivkin, "How Did Apple Computer Get Its Brand Name?" http://www.brandingstrategyinsider.com/2011/11/how-did-apple-computer-get-its-brand-name.html#.WD9ZS3eZM_M.

15 Don Fortner, "Sermon #1885 — Miscellaneous Sermons," http://www.donfortner.com/sermon_notes/01_genesis/gen%2003v22-24%20The%20Man%20is%20Become%20as%20One%20of%20Us%201885.htm.

16 University of Southern California, "Habits," https://dornsife.usc.edu/wendywood/habits.

17 Alan Deutschman, "Change or Die," https://www.fastcompany.com/52717/change-or-die.

18 Donald Miller, "How to Tell a Good Story With Your Life – or – The Four Critical Elements of a Meaningful Life," http://storylineblog.com/2012/03/06/how-to-tell-a-good-story-with-your-life.